MISCHIEF MARKETING

HOW THE RICH, FAMOUS & SUCCESSFUL
REALLY GOT THEIR CAREERS AND BUSINESSES GOING
(AND HOW YOU CAN, TOO!)

RAY SIMON

CB

CONTEMPORARY BOOKS

Library of Congress Cataloging-in-Publication Data

Simon, Ray.
     Mischief marketing / Ray Simon.
        p.   cm.
     Includes bibliographical references and index.
     ISBN 0-8092-2590-5
      1. Marketing.   I. Title.
   HF5415.S4968   2000
   658.8—dc21
                                                    00-22991
                                                     CIP

Cover design by Kim Bartko
Cover and interior illustration copyright © Adam McCauley
Interior design by Hespenheide Design

Published by Contemporary Books
A division of NTC/Contemporary Publishing Group, Inc.
4255 West Touhy Avenue, Lincolnwood (Chicago), Illinois 60712-1975 U.S.A.
Printed in the United States of America
International Standard Book Number: 0-8092-2590-5

00 01 02 03 04 05 MV 15 14 13 12 11 10 9 8 7 6 5 4 3 2 1

In memory of George Simon, the most

brilliant mischief marketer I've ever

known; and for future mischief marketers

Julie Shira and Matthew Adam Simon.

CONTENTS

ACKNOWLEDGMENTS

In *All About Eve*, there is a scene in which Eve, an actress whose ambition overshadows her talent, accepts a film award and dutifully thanks her colleagues in the audience—each of whom she has screwed over in some way during the course of her career. Demurely, she calls out each person's name to dispense platitudes and gratitudes. Disdainfully, each glares back, looks down, or snorts. Tough room.

I hope my acknowledgments are more sincere than Eve's, and will be better received by the people on my list. These people know me all too well, however, so my chances of coming off any better than Eve are not very good. But, anyway—having fastened my seat belt—here goes.

I'd like to thank Anthony Bernal for his incredible thoroughness and incalculably great and original contributions to the book; Ruth Dashosh, for sitting me down at her kitchen table one day and urging me to become a writer; Danielle Egan-Miller, for infusing logic and structure into a book that, without her relentless editorial defibrillations ("Clearer!"), would essentially have been a beat-era nightclub experiment in aleatory digression; Sheree Bykofsky, for being so cool to work with; Catherine Couture, for repeatedly hauling me back from the brink of lunatic pomposity; Emilio Segares, for sharing his formidable expertise on the soul-sapping horrors involved in doing even "pop" creative work; Bill Rosenblum, for teasing me when I needed teasing; Nola Hague and Robert Walter, for sharing valuable expertise about the publishing industry; Liesbeth Matthieu, for saying kind things at key moments; Dr. Ted Brandhurst, for providing many valuable suggestions, and for commiserating with me on the days of whines and poses that visit me far too often; Chuck DuPree, for E-mailing uncannily apt articles; Paul Addington Phipps, for contributing fascinating stuff about mischief marketing in the music industry; Monica Farrington, for expressing such enthusiasm about the book that even I would sometimes get excited; Wes Carpenter, Everette Gifford, Tom Benton, Tim Hall, and Ernie Boudreau, for being my favorite spiritual-giant-type gurus; my kids Shira and Matthew Simon, for putting up with Dad's workaholism; and finally Katie Couture, in her (noneditorial) role as soulmate and Official Gudgie-Wudgie, for riding this roller coaster of a life with me, even though she hates roller coasters.

WHAT IS MISCHIEF MARKETING?

> *A free-market capitalist system cannot operate fully effectively unless all participants in the economy are given opportunities to achieve their best. If we succeed in opening up opportunities to everyone, our national affluence will almost surely become more widespread.*
>
> —ALAN GREENSPAN
> "Maintaining Economic Viability"
> Speech for the Ford Museum Millennium Lecture Series,
> September 8, 1999

> *What?*
>
> —Martha to George in Edward Albee's *Who's Afraid of Virginia Woolf?*

Suppose you want to start a business—or sell your poetry or music, or wake people up to a social injustice—but you have no connections and no money? Or suppose you *have* money and connections but can't get the attention of a particular market or group of people? Or—here's an unusual scenario that's showing up more often—suppose you disdain marketing or are targeting a media-saturated audience composed of people who disdain marketing?

How do you accomplish your mission? How do you get your message across?

Well, it turns out that many successful people have marketed their offerings to the world using unusual strategies that go well beyond "guerrilla" marketing. There are more such people than you might think, they're a lot more famous than you might think, and they've been far more successful at using bizarre marketing tactics than you might think, too. They simply tend not to advertise what they've done. You wouldn't, either, if you were in their shoes.

No other book has been written exclusively about this approach to marketing (and, indeed, to life). That's why it needs a new name and a new treatment. We call it *mischief marketing*.

Take a look at these instances:

★ A prospective filmmaker sneaks onto the lot of Universal Studios and sets himself up in an empty office on the premises. He even buys some plastic letters and mounts his name in the building directory. The security guards greet him every morning. They think he belongs there. Eventually, his mischief marketing pays off. Studio executives view his first film, and, impressed, they grant him his first directing break. From there, he goes on to become the most successful director in the history of the film industry.

   The seventeen-year-old prospective filmmaker's name? Steven Spielberg.

★ An aspiring singer shows up at a Broadway audition. Shy and clumsy, she can't seem to do anything right. She chatters nervously, and her shoes don't even match. To make matters worse, she's chewing gum. When the moment comes for her to perform, she crudely spits out her gum and sticks it under the seat of a chair. Then she sings.

   Her raw talent and the sheer power of her voice mesmerize everyone in the theater. After she leaves, the auditioner decides to follow a hunch and inspect the chair. No trace of gum.

   That "shy" singer's name? Barbra Streisand.

★ An unkempt man seeking venture capital for a radically new business shows up at important meetings barefoot. At last, in concert with their shrewd observations about his odd new product, the investors conclude that he knows what he's doing, even if he is a nut. Indeed, they conclude he's a genius. He gets the resources he needs.

   That unkempt man's name? Steve Jobs, cofounder of Apple Computer.

★ A rebellious teenager wants to express in the media his deeply held convictions about religious hypocrisy, women's rights, male chauvinism, and a host of other topics, many of them infuriating to certain people who set themselves up as the guardians of moral virtue. Luckily, he has access to an important Boston newspaper. Unluckily, the paper is run by his brother, James, who wouldn't dream of publishing anything written by the teen.

So the boy uses a mischievous strategy to market his ideas. He slips under James's door a well-written article that seems to come from an articulate, independent young feminist named Silence Dogood. The tactic works, and James eventually ends up publishing not just that first piece, but thirteen subsequent—and very popular—works authored not by Silence Dogood, but his own seventeen-year-old brother. Eventually, one of these brilliant works contributes to the establishment of the First Amendment, protecting freedom of the press and of religion.

That mischievous teenager's name? Benjamin Franklin.

Would you like to know how the multimillionaire founder of a high-tech business was once so broke he had to get his friends to scurry around a rented office so the company would look busy? I'll tell you the whole engaging story. I'll also showcase tales about Fortune 500 business leaders—Bill Gates, Ted Turner, Ben and Jerry—who still use mischievous strategies to grow and nurture their companies.

Would you like to know how Mother Teresa of Calcutta turned a simple airline lunch into perhaps thousands of dollars for the poor (and valuable publicity for her cause) just by strategically asking a few peculiar questions? That, too, is within the scope of *Mischief Marketing*, because mischief marketing is as much about the marketing of ideas and values as it is about money and careers.

Many of the anecdotes you'll see in these pages will act as templates. In other words, they'll illustrate by example how you can adapt the strategies embodied in the tales to fit your own situation; how you can tailor the tales and the tactics to fit your own business, personal, or social goals. In fact, I'll sometimes call these stories "templative tales" because they're worth reflecting upon, or *contemplating*, and because they can act as templates for developing your own mischief marketing strategies.

For instance, it might not be your style to break into a movie studio. That's understandable. But there are similar things you can do to accomplish what the Spielberg templative tale is essentially about: evoking an aura of credibility. On the Internet, for example, you could craft a website that is as impressive as any produced by a major corporation, and such a website can do for you what the mischievously makeshift office at Universal Studios did for Spielberg.

Or take the Streisand story. Is that a prescription to act like a klutz in front of people you want to impress? Not at all. Klutziness is only incidentally what the tale is about. The Streisand story is *essentially* about how to sequence your presentation mischievously and creatively, so that your audience's expectations are lowered. (It is not until you're well into *Jaws* that you get even a glimpse of the shark, remember?) In other words, this deliberate orchestration of expectations paves the way for you to shock your prospects later with the unexpected excellence of what follows.

The point is, this is not just a book of fascinating stories about kooky things famous people did to get started. This is a book of essential *techniques* and effective *strategies* that you can apply to your marketing, even if you're marketing not a product or service, but just a wholesome value to your kids, such as the value of education, the value of free speech in a democracy, or the value (as in Mother Teresa's case) of helping the poor.

Because some of these tactics are obviously controversial, this is also a book that will require you to read between the lines. I'm sorry to be so cryptic, but it's true. If you read this book carefully, you'll learn much more than you expected to learn about many things that may or may not have to do with marketing as we know it.

Definition of Mischief Marketing

Sometimes it helps to give a formal, dictionary-style definition of any new field of study like mischief marketing. And sometimes it succeeds only in making an author look like a fatuous jerk. I'll take a chance and go with a dictionary-type definition.

> Mischief Marketing \'mis-chef marketing\ *n* (14c. Middle
> English *meschief*, from Old French, from *mes-* + *chief* (head, end)
> + marketing) 1: a type of marketing that uses highly unorthodox,
> often humorous, and sometimes barely legal strategies for reaching precisely targeted prospects 2: the title of the first book to collect a significant amount of information about such unorthodox marketing practices in one place; to document it; to distinguish mischief marketing from hoaxes, public relations stunts, and similar phenemona; and to outline a program for designing and conducting one's own mischief marketing campaigns; written by a fatuous twenty-first century author.

What Is an Offering?

As you have no doubt noticed, mischief marketing broadens the definition of an "offering" to a "prospect." It means selling a product to a customer, of course, but it could also mean getting the IRS to resolve a tax problem for you, winning a statewide election, getting your music heard or your art displayed, raising the nation's consciousness about civil rights or consumer abuses, motivating your spouse to pay more attention to you, persuading your kids to do their chores, or even winning the heart of a soul mate.

That's why, instead of talking about "selling" we use the generic expression "making an offering to a prospect." It can apply to anything from a business venture to a spiritual teaching. Incidentally, one of the earliest meanings of the word "offering" can be found in the Bible. For religious people, the ultimate "prospect" for your offering is You-Know-Who upstairs.

Some Hand-Picked Facts About Mischief Marketing

★ Mischief marketing is not only about how to market products and services. It is equally about how to promote concepts and values (such as racial and gender equality or equal economic opportunity) in the marketplace of ideas.

★ Mischief marketing is similar to guerrilla marketing in some ways, but it is really designed for the guerrilla's guerrilla.

★ Many famous people have used mischief marketing to jump-start their careers. They just don't talk about it much to the public, for obvious reasons.

★ Mischief marketing is not usually about marketing to masses of people (although it can be). It's usually about marketing to specific VLPs—very leveraged persons. Of course, such VLPs may themselves have influence over mass markets, and to the extent that they do, you could say mischief marketing is *indirectly* about reaching mass markets. But it is not primarily about that. It is primarily about reaching leveraged individuals, or relatively small, leveraged groups.

★ In mischief marketing, a small, leveraged group could have anywhere from 5 to 540 members, or more. Congress, for example, is a relatively small, highly leveraged group.

Many Trips to the John, Son

The following historical snippet is about a twenty-two-year-old giant with big ears. Two weeks earlier, the young man had been teaching high school in Houston, Texas. Now, as secretary to a member of Congress, he was already inching his way (mischievously) toward becoming president of the United States.

[H]is first night at the Dodge [Hotel in Washington, D.C.], he did something strange, something he would admit to biographer and intimate Doris Kearns in the months just before he died. That night, Lyndon Baines Johnson took four showers. Four times he walked towel-draped to the communal bathroom down along the hall. Four times he turned on the water and lathered up. The next morning he got up early to brush his teeth five times, with five-minute intervals in between.

The young man from Texas had a mission. There were seventy-five other congressional secretaries living in the building. He wanted to meet as many of them as possible as fast as possible.

The strategy worked. Within three months of arriving in Washington, the new-

★ Mischief marketing is both as old as the hills and brand-spanking new. Old as the hills because mischievous strategies have been used for centuries—especially whenever the gap between the haves and the have-nots (or the gender gap) has been too big to bridge by normal means. Brand-spanking new because, until recently, nobody isolated and defined mischief marketing as a distinct phenomenon.

Other famous people who have used mischief marketing strategies to market ideas, products, or services include:

★ Ted Turner
★ President George Washington
★ Mae West
★ The Bee Gees
★ President Lyndon B. Johnson
★ Physicist Alan Sokal
★ Will Rogers
★ Comedian Andy Kaufman
★ Hunter Thompson
★ Steve Jobs
★ Duke Ellington
★ Bishop Jacques Gaillot
★ Orson Welles
★ Random House founder Bennett Cerf
★ Andy Warhol
★ Mathematician Sophie Germain
★ Coco Chanel
★ Habitat for Humanity founder Millard Fuller
★ Elton John
★ P. T. Barnum
★ Walt Whitman
★ Winery founder Walter Taylor
★ Estee Lauder
★ President John F. Kennedy
★ Jazz clarinetist Mezz Mezzrow
★ Borland founder Philippe Kahn

★ Harrison Ford
★ Ice-cream moguls Ben and Jerry

You may be thinking that the definition I just supplied includes something about "barely legal strategies." Is this stuff cheating? Is it trickery? Does it have a note of chicanery? Is it a sin? Let's consult a higher authority on this matter.

> *Self-aggrandizement, of course, is a business as old as mankind itself. In the book of Judges, God told Gideon to ramp up only 300 soldiers—so long as they all blew rams' horns and carried torches. Scared the sandals off 135,000 Midianites.*
>
> —DAN MORSE
> *Wall Street Journal*
> December 7, 1998

comer got himself elected Speaker of the "Little Congress," the organization of all House staff assistants.

—CHRISTOPHER MATTHEWS
Hardball: How Politics Is Played—Told by One Who Knows the Game
Summit Books, 1988

Idea Joggers

- What can *you* do to casually make yourself seem familiar to potentially helpful people?
- The people you want to meet—where do they hang out? Can you go to these places and be seen there? Can you make friends there?

What Mischief Marketing Is Not

Almost every new idea—if it's any good—is confusing at first. This is because nearly every novel concept hovers close to other, older ideas to which we're more accustomed. This proximity to related ideas makes it easy to get the new concept mixed up with the old ones.

Remember when you learned the alphabet? The letter *d* looked a lot like the letter *b*, *p* looked like *q*, and so on. Many different letters so closely resembled each other that it took a while to tell them apart, didn't it? We had to learn that one letter may resemble—but is *not*—the other.

Before we dive into the deep end of the pool, let's look at what mischief marketing may

Mischief Marketing in Nature— Coloration

*M*ost animals need both concealment and advertisement. An animal may need to conceal itself from predators and to advertise its presence to symbionts or to members of its own species for reproductive purposes.

Many birds that conceal courtship coloration when their feathers are held close to the body present a brilliant display upon erecting their feathers. Similar mechanisms are common in many animals, such as Anolis lizards, which have brightly coloured throat fans that are visible only when erected during courtship or threat behaviour. . . . Some predators deceive with advertising coloration.

—"COLORATION"
Encyclopædia
Britannica Online

resemble, but is not. Once we're able to discern the differences, all the material that follows will make sense, just as the letters on this page now make sense because you know the alphabet.

Mischief Marketing Is Not About Publicity Stunts

Publicity stunts are not tailored to specific individuals, groups, or corporations. They represent scattershot bids for media attention—the marketing equivalent of a desperate drunk at a single's bar. But we don't want a prospect to see us flinging ourselves at the first sailor who glances in our direction. We want them to observe instead that we're thoughtful, meticulous, daring, and effective; that we're creative problem solvers in control of our agenda.

Mischief marketing campaigns, therefore, are painstakingly customized and microtargeted. In essence, they're business courtships. Designed to attract the attention of specific individuals or small groups of people, mischief marketing campaigns in their ideal form are subtle and personal. Publicity stunts are never subtle, and seldom personal.

Mischief Marketing Is Not About Tricking People

E-mail spammers try to get you to read their get rich quick messages by hiding them under deceptive subject headers ("Thinking of You"). Direct mailers try to con you into opening their pieces by making them look like subpoenas ("Time-Sensitive Documents").

Mischief marketing has nothing whatever to do with bait-and-switch schemes. In mischief marketing, you're establishing a relationship with your prospect. And as with any relationship, you don't want to make false promises just to get yourself into bed with some company. If you do that, your façade will eventually crumble, and you'll be left alone with your miracle bra or toupee in hand. If what you're after is a lasting relationship, you need to be authentic.

A mischief marketing campaign is always sensitive to its intended recipients and always respects their intelligence, their privacy, and the value of their time. It is a seduction of the highest order.

And think about it: who doesn't want to feel special? Who doesn't revel in the fact that some stranger has taken the time to discover what we're really like, what we really need and want, what will make us smile? Don't we all want that?

Mischief Marketing Tip:

Make it fun. Mischief marketing should be a pleasurable experience for both the marketer and the marketee.

Mischief Marketing Is Not About Lying to People

One of the most important mischief marketing commandments (Chapter 9) is "Thou shalt not lie." You can legitimately present the truth in its best possible light—albeit a light that is carefully lensed and precisely angled. Indeed, that's what the Vulcan tactic in Chapter 12 is all about. And come to think of it, that's what most movie stars are all about.

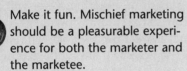

Movie stars have fans at their throats. Anolis lizards have throat fans. So there you go.

—UTA ELLISATT

He Never Told a Lie, but He Sure Could Spin Some Yarn

*L*et's pause for a moment to think about America's founding fathers. These revolutionaries were not above dabbling in mischief when the ends justified the means.

[George Washington] had, despite his own misgivings about a lack of education, a sense of his own worth and a theatrical flair for impressing others. Even as a young colonial militiaman, he had designed his special uniform. As a civilian at Mount Vernon, he summoned Charles Wilson Peale to paint him wearing it. When the time came to choose a colonial commander in chief of the military, Washington declared his availability by appearing uniformed in Philadelphia.

> —GARRY WILLS
> *Certain Trumpets: The Call of Leaders*
> Simon & Schuster, 1994

Idea Joggers

- What can you do to state symbolically that you *already are* what you want to be?
- Can you get someone else—as Washington got

(continued)

Peale—to put a "seal of approval" on your new image by making an artistic or symbolic object out of it—something that instantly lends an aura of credibility (and inevitability)?

In other words, it's okay to present things in a good light. But if you want your effort to qualify as an authentic mischief marketing campaign, telling lies is simply out of bounds.

Mischief Marketing Is Not About Misrepresenting Your Offering

In huge letters, the sweepstakes envelope says you have already won ten million dollars. In small letters, it says, ". . . *if* you return the winning numbers."

Mischief marketing has nothing to do with petty stupidity like this. Ideally, it is never insulting or disappointing. And even if a mischief marketing campaign does appear to be insulting at first, the superb mischief marketer will always strive to correct that impression later. In authentic mischief marketing, the joke will always be revealed. The hoax will always be exposed.

Mischief Marketing Tip:

Always deliver more. A mischief marketing campaign always respects people, and always delivers more—never less—than what it promises.

Mischief Marketing Is Not About Hassling People

Recently, some guy tried to attract the attention of a film director by doing a silly performance in front of the security cameras at the gates to the director's home. The guy was, of course, arrested and hauled off to jail—as he should have been. If a stranger were to stand outside your happy home and do an insane little number when you answered the door, would you invite him in or would you call 911? Yeah, I thought so.

What Mischief Marketing Is Not

P. T. Barnum sometimes crossed the line from mischief marketing into chicanery.

But in fairness to the crazy, old bas—er, I mean, in fairness to the old master, you could charitably consider the following story to be about what we nowadays call "internship."

When a trumpet-player applied to Barnum for a job in the band, he was surprised to be hired on the spot. But when he had received no salary for several weeks, he was even more surprised. He approached the young showman. "Pay!" boomed Barnum. "I pay you? Nothing of the sort. You are to pay me. You seem not to understand, my young friend, that my band is made up of men who are learning their instruments, and want a good outdoor place for practice and to get the hang of playing together. They are glad enough to pay, and of course they ought to be, for there is no such chance in America for an industrious musician to advance in his art as in the band of Barnum's great American Museum.

> —IRVING WALLACE
> *The Fabulous Showman: The Life and Times of P. T. Barnum*
> Knopf, 1959

Idea Joggers

- Barnum's behavior in this story is questionable, of course. But aren't there legitimate ways of doing this kind of thing?
- For example, can you inspire people to work for low pay on your project—then amply reward them later by giving them stock options or a share of your profits?

- Can you set up a work-study program? That is, can you teach people new and valuable skills, while enlisting them to help you with your projects in exchange?
- If you're mischief marketing an idea, can you inspire volunteers to perceive the intrinsic value of doing good works?

More on What Mischief Marketing Is Not

*L*et's inspect the following story and then specify exactly why it is *not* a mischief marketing story.

Early one morning, investors who were reading the finance message boards hosted by Yahoo were surprised by a posting headlined "Buyout News." The message claimed that PairGain Technologies had agreed to be acquired by ECI Telecom in a deal valued at over a billion dollars. A hyperlink embedded in the text led surfers to what seemed to be a news article by Bloomberg, a respected provider of financial data. Naturally, trading in PairGain's shares immediately took off.

Unfortunately, as many learned by lunchtime, the whole thing was a hoax.

(continued)

What made it convincing (it fooled a number of otherwise savvy investors) was that the Web page supposedly representing the Bloomberg article even included a banner ad, hyperlinks to actual Bloomberg pages, and an overall look and feel that precisely matched what regular viewers of Bloomberg's site were used to seeing.

Here are just a few reasons why this is not a mischief marketing story:

- It involves outright misrepresentation or lying (commandment 4).
- The author did not expose the hoax him- or herself (commandment 13).
- The mischief irritated the prospects (commandment 2).
- The offering was not superb because there was no offering at all (commandment 1).
- Apart from violating these commandments, it failed to be humorous and failed to deliver more than it promised.

One of the mischief marketing commandments is "Thou shalt not irritate thy prospect." This means you cannot interrupt your prospect at a restaurant while he or she is enjoying dinner. You cannot go to his or her home. You cannot deposit strange packages on the prospect's doorstep. You cannot accost him or her on the street or call at odd hours. Did you see *Fatal Attraction*? Picture that film in the context of business. Not good.

If you do things like this, you're not engaging in mischief marketing; you're just harassing people and making a fool of yourself. You don't want to do that sort of thing. It's not you.

In short, an authentic mischief marketing project is always:

★ positive
★ upbeat
★ clever
★ light
★ engaging
★ elegant
★ respectful
★ precisely tailored
★ well planned
★ meticulously executed

Now that you've seen what mischief marketing is—and isn't—let's find out how it can benefit you as no other form of marketing can.

How Can Mischief Marketing Benefit You?

What are the benefits of mischief marketing? What good is it? Under what conditions does it work better than conventional marketing? Is mischief marketing for you, or for your company? Let's start with the last question first.

Is Mischief Marketing Right for You?

The following quiz will help you figure out whether or not mischief marketing is your cup of tea, and what you can get out of it.

1. Are you struggling so hard to get started in your chosen field that you're nearly ready to give up on the American Dream altogether?
    Is your situation like Streisand's? She had lousy prospects for being a star, mostly because she was so funny looking (Broadway producer David Merrick called her ugly). With the help of some mischievous marketing, however, she overcame her limitations. So can you.

2. Are you having a hard time starting a new career or changing careers?
    Actor Kimberlee Elizabeth Kramer wanted to change careers because her age (thirty-two) made it hard for her to get good acting jobs. She decided to try launching a new career as a writer with a Disney-affiliated TV show called "Felicity."
    Nobody should care how old a writer is, right? That's what Kimberlee figured.

But apparently, Disney associates and affiliates weren't any keener on thirty-two-year-old writers than they were on thirty-two-year-old actors. So Kramer had to do a little mischief marketing to get the job.

With the help of her ex-husband, she continued doing something she had already done as an actor—telling people she was only nineteen. Sure enough, she got the writing job on "Felicity." But the story doesn't end there.

When Disney discovered her true age, the company tried to fire her, and the whole age bias fiasco somehow made it into many major newspapers. "This is one of the great ruses in television" said one network executive.

Disney did not like this media coverage. It had already suffered from bad press alleging dreadful hiring practices and miserable treatment of employees. In any case, the hoopla eventually died down, everyone kissed and made up, and all is well today with Kimberlee in her new career.

Is your situation like this? Then you need mischief marketing.

3. Are you a journalist or concerned citizen who'd like to expose injustice, fraud, or corruption (maybe on the part of your competitor) without jeoparizing your life and the lives of your family members?

Jeffrey Wigand (whose story is told in *The Insider*) was a key witness in the exposé of tobacco industry corruption. The reward for his courage, however, was that his everyday life became hellish. But if he had used the mischievous, risk-minimizing DRUID and FIAT communication tactics discussed in Chapter 6, he could have exercised his freedom of speech, exposed the tobacco companies, and spared himself a lot of pain and misery.

Incidentally, do you know how "60 Minutes" got around a legal muzzle that stopped it from running an important story on tobacco industry corruption? By using the mischievous device of reporting about how it "could not report" the story. If you want to know more about doing that sort of thing yourself, mischief marketing is for you.

4. Are you a corporate honcho who's been struggling without success to crack a finicky market or age group (like Gen X-ers, for example)?

The makers of Miller Lite did some research that revealed that their beer appealed mostly to older, conservative people. Miller wanted to appeal to younger people, too, but the new market was not as easy to penetrate as the company had hoped it would be. Miller did something creative and wacky (they tried to parody their own marketing) but it was not genuine mischief marketing. Had it done *genuine* mischief marketing, the campaign might have worked.

5. Are you frustrated because you don't have enough connections, "juice," or money to get your business going?

     Are you like Philippe Kahn, who had miserable prospects for starting a software business because he didn't have any money? Or are you like Lyndon Johnson, who arrived in Washington with no friends and no connections? Both used mischief marketing to transcend their shortcomings.

Mischief marketing will help you enormously, or at least amuse you, if you can recognize yourself in any of the following descriptions:

★ You're a creative individual who needs to market a unique product or service.
★ You're bored with conventional techniques.
★ You hate marketing and selling, but you know you have to do it in order to survive in this golden-calf-worshipping world.
★ You want to expose injustice or corruption in business or politics or you want to expose a competitor's injustices.
★ You're a shy person who'd like to get a meeting with someone you find intimidating or inaccessible.
★ You're an artist, musician, or performer.
★ You don't care *what* it's about—you just want to do something *different* for a change!

Perspectives on Mischief Marketing

To discuss the benefits and qualities of mischief marketing more thoroughly, let's use a communication tool that dates back to Plato—the dialogue. Let's eavesdrop on a conversation between four people whose divergent perspectives will help us see what mischief marketing is all about.

CORPORATE CHARLIE: a down-to-earth, numbers-oriented guy who works in the marketing department of a giant corporation.

INOFFENSIVE IAN: a somewhat creative person, but one who believes that everything in marketing should be safe, cute, and inoffensive.

MISCHIEVOUS MARIE: our heroine.

MARCUS AURELIUS: Roman emperor (A.D. 120–180)

CORPORATE CHARLIE: Marie, I don't understand. Aren't you essentially talking about *publicity stunts* with this whole mischief marketing thing?

MISCHIEVOUS MARIE: Not at all. I've said this before, but I'll say it again: Publicity stunts are things you do for the mass media, for newspapers and TV stations. But mischief marketing is usually directed at particular individuals, or at very specific, *microtargeted* groups of people. Look at Steven Spielberg's story, for instance. You can see that he wasn't interested in getting on TV or seeing his name in the papers. He was interested in engaging a particular group of people—namely, the people who work in the movie business. He wanted to meet them and learn from them, so he used mischief marketing to get in the door.

CORPORATE CHARLIE: But breaking into a movie studio, as Spielberg did, or posing as a woman as Benjamin Franklin did—jeez, why would someone like me need to use such bizarre tactics? I work for a corporation that has millions of dollars to spend on advertising. We don't need to do oddball stuff like that. Using tried and true techniques, and armies of focus groups and statisticians, we can reach any group of people we want to reach.

MISCHIEVOUS MARIE: Can you? But big-budget advertising just doesn't work on everyone, does it? Lots of people are wise to advertising. They're even wise to focus groups. They know all the tricks. It's not like the old days, back in the 1950s, say, when you could just make some proclamation on TV ("We're the best!") and everyone in Pleasantville would believe you. People don't trust advertising anymore. If there ever was someone who should have learned about mischief marketing a long time ago, oh, it was you, Charlie. It was you.

MARCUS AURELIUS: Outward things can touch the soul not a whit. They know no way into it. They have no power to sway or move it. By itself it sways and moves itself.

MISCHIEVOUS MARIE: Exactly.

CORPORATE CHARLIE: *(Glancing at Emperor Aurelius)* O-kay.

INOFFENSIVE IAN: Marie, why is it called mischief marketing? Why not call it subversive marketing? It sounds subversive, maybe even a little sneaky, don't you think? Subversive . . . stealthy . . . I *love* it. *(Giggles.)*

MISCHIEVOUS MARIE: Well, the word "subversive" implies an element of secrecy. Sometimes mischief marketing involves secrecy, but it's more often aboveboard. Take the story of how Clorox got on its feet. The company was once so broke that the owners could afford to make only watered-down bleach instead of the industrial-strength stuff they wanted to sell. But it turned out that a whole bunch of customers wanted the cheaper, watered-down bleach more than they wanted the heavy-duty bleach. Why? Because the cheaper bleach worked for doing laundry. Of course, it was mischievous of Clorox, at first, to give away free samples of weak bleach. But they weren't subversive about it. They weren't secretive. They didn't misrepresent anything. They simply tried out a rather offbeat, mischievous idea—and it worked.

Or look at Mother Teresa. Everything she did was up front. There was never any subterfuge involved in her "marketing" work. But what she did was still mischievous. For instance, she once stood in a line with her groceries and simply waited for someone to foot the bill—which someone finally did. There was no subterfuge involved, yet it was a mischievous thing to do.

CORPORATE CHARLIE: But Clorox shouldn't have used such techniques. What they should have done instead was spend millions of dollars for advertising. Then they should have made up a catchy jingle and hired Michael Jordan. Then they should have . . .

INOFFENSIVE IAN: *(Leaping to his feet.)* Right! And in their multimillion-dollar prime-time TV ads they should have featured dancing bottles of full-strength Clorox! Oh, I just *love* a lively, dancing cartoon figure, don't you? They're so unique. So creative. And fun!

CORPORATE CHARLIE: So how would a big corporation use mischief marketing?

MISCHIEVOUS MARIE: I don't like big corporations, Charlie. They ruin everything. Look at how they're trying to ruin the Internet. As one of the Net's elder statesmen, David Farber, once put it: "The danger is that there is an overwhelming desire among corporations to turn [the Internet] into something they understand, and defeat all the marvelous potential of it."

CORPORATE CHARLIE: Marie, you're on your Kennedy-era, leftist bandwagon again, and you know it.

INOFFENSIVE IAN: Now now, children. No fighting. No arguing. Play nice.

MISCHIEVOUS MARIE: Okay, okay. A few big corporations are already using mischief marketing. They just don't call it that.

CORPORATE CHARLIE: Marie, are you going to give me an example of how a corporation like mine would use mischief marketing?

MISCHIEVOUS MARIE: Sure. Suppose you're with a big company (or a tiny one, for that matter) and you decide you want Ralph Nader to endorse your product. He isn't motivated by money, so you couldn't just buy his testimony outright. How would you reach out to him? After all, if you could get a very leveraged person like Nader to be your spokesperson, your product would acquire instant credibility, wouldn't it? But the only way to persuade someone like that to endorse you would be to conduct a precisely targeted campaign directed toward him as an individual. In other words— to do mischief marketing.

INOFFENSIVE IAN: Yes! I see what you mean! Maybe you could dress up in a clown suit and go to Nader's office! That should do it! And you could do that song! *(Sings with deep feeling.)* "Isn't it rich / Are we a pair."

MARCUS AURELIUS: *(Brooding.)* How many who came into this world with me have already left it!

CORPORATE CHARLIE: Now it sounds like you're talking about marketing yourself to a powerful spokesperson or endorser. Am I getting warmer with this whole microtargeting concept?

MISCHIEVOUS MARIE: Yes, if by a spokesperson or endorser you mean a very leveraged person—someone who can influence a larger market.

CORPORATE CHARLIE: Okay. That makes sense. But Marie, we already know how to get endorsers, or VLPS, or whatever you want to call them. We do it all the time. Why, we got Bill Shatner just last year. We can get anyone we want!

MISCHIEVOUS MARIE: Maybe. But not without paying them huge amounts of money.

CORPORATE CHARLIE: Well, how else are you going to snare VLPS?

MISCHIEVOUS MARIE: Would you say the attorney general is a very credible, very leveraged person? Perhaps more so than even Bill Shatner? What do you think you'd have to pay to, as you say, "snare" her endorsement for you?

CORPORATE CHARLIE: Well, you probably couldn't pay her any actual money—not outright, anyway. It would probably be against the law.

Mischievous Marie: And yet there *is* a company that mischievously got Attorney General Janet Reno to act, in effect, as its spokesperson without having to pay her a nickel.

Corporate Charlie: What company was that?

Mischievous Marie: Netscape, of course. By persuading the attorney general to take up the case against Microsoft, rival Netscape along with other companies did an end run around Microsoft's marketing juggernaut and captured more brand awareness than they could have generated even if they'd had *twice* the advertising budget of Microsoft. In other words, they leveraged their contact with one person—or with just a handful of people at the Justice Department—into a contact with millions of regular folks.

Corporate Charlie: But didn't their suit have merit?

Mischievous Marie: Certainly, but that's not the point, Charles. The point is that no matter what merit the suit did or didn't have, it gave them lots of marketing mileage for very little money.

Corporate Charlie: Hmm. I see. And you say this was mischief marketing?

Mischievous Marie: Well, it certainly wasn't *conventional* marketing, Charles.

Corporate Charlie: The tone, Marie. Watch the tone.

Marcus Aurelius: When you are outraged by somebody's impudence, ask yourself at once, "Can the world exist without impudent people?" It cannot; so do not ask for impossibilities.

Mischievous Marie: Right.

Big Punisher

Music industry experts agree that it was "street marketing"—a subset of mischief marketing—that contributed most heavily to rap artist Big Punisher's rise from obscurity to stardom.

Two full years before the release of his album, Big Pun's producer, Loud Records (partly owned by Bertelsmann AG'S RCA Records), started promoting him by sending out "street teams" to New York, Chicago, and Los Angeles.

Among other things, these mischievous teams spray-painted the rapper's name on sidewalks and traced out the words "Big Pun" in the dirt on parked trucks in Manhattan. This meant that the vehicles instantly (and at a dirt cheap price) became traveling billboards for Big Pun as they trundled their way through the city.

And so it happened that without major airplay, without a video on MTV, without coverage in Rolling Stone—in short, without the help of any of the promotional strategies held sacrosanct by the pop and rock marketing establishment—*Capital Punishment* soon became the fifth-bestselling album in the country.

(continued)

Whereas phenomena such as Spice Girls were born of widespread, traditional public relations blitzes, the rapper launch is a murkier trajectory—starting first with the low-cost campaigns begun literally on street corners. And teams' inventive, sometimes illegal, marketing strategies—in evidence since the early '90s but now used on a far larger scale—are changing the ground rules of how pop music, not just rap, is promoted today.

—PATRICK M. REILLY
"Buddha at School: How 'Street Teams' Create Rap Sensations"
Wall Street Journal,
June 25, 1998

CORPORATE CHARLIE: Let me ask you something else, Marie. You say mischief marketing is mostly about marketing creatively to a single, leveraged person, or to a small group of leveraged people, right?

MISCHIEVOUS MARIE: Right.

CORPORATE CHARLIE: But don't *some* stories in this book represent nothing more than cheap publicity stunts?

MISCHIEVOUS MARIE: Such as?

CORPORATE CHARLIE: Such as the story about how Big Punisher's record company wrote his name all over trucks.

MISCHIEVOUS MARIE: Okay. Great story. What are you trying to say?

CORPORATE CHARLIE: I'm saying that Big Pun's marketing campaign was just a publicity stunt. It wasn't targeted to a particular leveraged group or to a particular person, so you can't call it mischief marketing.

MISCHIEVOUS MARIE: *(Sighing.)* Maybe you're right, Charlie. Maybe that particular story is about a publicity stunt, except for the fact that it wasn't designed to attract the attention of the press at all. I suppose you could say it wasn't precisely targeted to street kids who distrust marketing. You *could* say it was just a stunt.

CORPORATE CHARLIE: *(Triumphant.)* So, that Big Pun story is *not* about mischief marketing, then, is it? True or false?

MISCHIEVOUS MARIE: Charlie, tell me. Is the story behind *The Blair Witch Project* true or false? The horror film was made on a

tiny budget and shocked corporate Hollywood when it became hugely successful at the box office almost exclusively through mischief
marketing.

CORPORATE CHARLIE: Well, as I recall, the filmmakers kept everything ambiguous at first. They didn't tell you whether the spooky story was true or false.

MISCHIEVOUS MARIE: Right. Ambiguity is a very powerful tactic in the mischief marketing repertoire.

CORPORATE CHARLIE: So? What has that got to do with Big Pun? I asked you whether the stuff Big Pun did was just a PR stunt, or whether it was genuine mischief marketing. Why can't I ever get a straight answer from you? I don't like ambiguity. *I want a formula!* I want to be able to pin this thing down like a butterfly to a corkboard!

MISCHIEVOUS MARIE: Too bad, sweetie.

MARCUS AURELIUS: Unless things pertain to a man, as a man, they cannot properly be said to belong to him. They cannot be required of him, for . . .

CORPORATE CHARLIE: Okay. Okay. Just tell me more about how mischief marketing can help big corporations.

MISCHIEVOUS MARIE: Mischief marketing was not meant to help big corporations. I hope you and your corporate cronies never catch on to mischief marketing. Mischief marketing is for poor people, for people who are at a disadvantage in life, for creative people who have problems trying to get started in life, for square pegs trying to fit into round holes. And you know, when I first met you— before you sold out shamelessly to your big, fancy corporation— that was you, too, Charlie.

CORPORATE CHARLIE: It was not.

MISCHIEVOUS MARIE: Oh, it was you, Charlie. It was you.

Mischievous Pop Quiz

1. Unlike PR-centered, conventional, or guerrilla marketing, mischief marketing is usually:
   a) microtargeted to specific individuals or small groups.
   b) a little nuts.
   c) primarily about having fun rather than just making money.
   d) all of the above.

2. In mischief marketing, a VLP is a:
   a) vicious legume popper.
   b) very leveraged person.
   c) variable-length penis.

3. Which of the following statements is true?
   a) Ambiguity is a powerful tactic in mischief marketing, and choice (b) is false.
   b) Ambiguity is a powerful tactic in mischief marketing, and choice (a) is true.
   c) Kurt Godel.

Scoping and Previewing Your Mischief Marketing Campaign

To picture how mischief marketing fits in with all the other kinds of marketing available, imagine a spectrum of prospects. For instance, think of the classic color spectrum that goes from infrared on the left through red, orange, yellow, green, blue, indigo, violet (remember ROYGBIV?), and ultraviolet on the right.

Mischief marketing works best on the left end of the spectrum. Totalitarian marketing (the kind preferred by the medieval Catholic church and by people like Stalin) works best on the right end. Everything else falls in the middle.

On the extreme left, you might picture just one particular individual to whom you're marketing your offering. That could be, say, a potential spouse. In that case, your offering is—just you. So your potential spouse could occupy the leftmost region of the band.

On the extreme right of the scale, picture some huge demographic such as China or the entire globe. This would represent the prospects Microsoft is after, for example. If you want to reach these prospects on the right (ultraviolet) end of this scale, you obviously can't use mischief marketing. It doesn't apply there. Instead, you'll need a huge advertising budget, hegemony over all distribution channels, control of the media, an air force, ground troops, political lobbyists, hordes of screaming fanatics, and so on.

This is the world of big business and "wag the dog" politics. It is the world in which you hire legions of lawyers to file patents and trademarks on the human genome, on the sky, or on water. It's the world about which conspiracy theorists go nuts, because to worry about massive things you can't control is the surest route to madness. The prospects are,

Loco Coco

Coco Chanel was a master at targeting a leveraged, well-defined group. And she learned early in her career that when you launch a new product, the way to make it alluring to rich socialites (a fairly well-defined group) is not just by asking them to pay a lot of money for it, but by allowing them to fancy that they played a key role in its conception and eventual success.

Here's a nicely mischievous story about how Chanel No. 5 got launched.

First, Coco got in touch with a perfume maker named Beaux and hired him to produce an extremely expensive perfume with lots of costly jasmine in it. She wanted it to be the most expensive perfume in the world.

Then Coco gathered up a few sample bottles of her new perfume, squirreled them back to Paris, and started offering them as gifts to her best clients. She also asked her sales clerks to atomize the fitting rooms in her dress shop with the new scent. When one of her clients would come back and ask how she could buy the perfume, Coco would feign surprise.

"Ah, the little vial I gave you the other day." She smiled. "My dear, I don't sell

quite simply, all human beings on earth. The only way a lone individual or small company could reach such prospects without massive resources would be to start a huge religious movement. For details on such a process, read and study biographies of Buddha, Moses, Jesus, Muhammad, Joseph Smith, and so on.

Adjacent to the infrared area (where your spouse is), somewhere around the red area, would be other family members. To these prospects, you would mischievously market ideas, of course, because you usually aren't selling products or services to your kids. How would you approach these prospects?

Well, to your teenage daughter, Shira, you might compose a volume very much like this one, in which you might say something like, "You know, I really hate to go through the hassle of writing and publishing a book—and a business book no less—simply to get this message across to you. But I wish you would clean up your room. Please? Jeez, where do you get your bad habits from? And clean up my messy office while you're at it, will ya?" This is just an arbitrary, totally fictional example, of course.

In the orange area of the spectrum, you'd have small, local businesses. You might want the owners of such businesses to become your clients, or you might want to use mischief marketing to get a job with one of them.

In the yellow area, you'd have larger companies. But even here, a mischief marketer will always want to locate *specific individuals* within those companies. With mischief marketing, you always try to address particular people, not masses. Even if your ultimate goal is to market to the masses, you would start by marketing to a particular individual or a small, well-defined group.

In sum, when dealing with a large company, always remember: no matter how huge an organization may be, it is run by actual, living human beings. These individuals are your real prospects if you want to market to people in the corporate region of the spectrum.

In the green and blue areas, the target market starts to get too big. Mischief marketing techniques won't work here by themselves. If you want to be effective in reaching these prospects, you'll need to combine guerrilla marketing, conventional marketing, and mischief marketing. In other words, you'll need to use conventional and guerrilla techniques to reach large numbers of people in this region of the spectrum and mischief marketing to reach influential individuals with tremendous leverage over markets, individuals like Oprah Winfrey, Barbara Walters, or Alan Greenspan.

In the indigo and violet areas, things start getting expensive. This is Madison Avenue's strip. You can't really use mischief marketing at all in this region unless you've already used it to get to the point where you can now call up Ted Turner, for example, and say, "Don't forget to bring home a quart of milk." There are people who operate mischievously at this level, primarily in order to market social and political ideas, but they tend to remain in the background. They found out that you can get a lot more accomplished wearing pop camouflage than you can using almost any other technique.

perfume. I found the little bottles almost by chance in Grasse, at a perfumer whose name I've forgotten. I thought it would be an original little gift for my friends."

The scene repeated itself as salesgirls kept vaporizing the fitting rooms and other "dear friends" who had been among the privileged to receive a little gift came back and recognized the perfume sample.

Coco bombarded Beaux with telegrams demanding that he accelerate the start-up of the production. With her clients she went to phase two of her campaign.

"You think I should have it made and sell it?" she asked. "You mean you really like my perfume?"

When Beaux announced he was in production, she had new lines for the clients. "Maybe you're right," or, "Yes, I followed your advice. I'll be getting the perfume you like so much."

—Axel Madsen
Chanel: A Woman of Her Own
Henry Holt, 1990

Idea Joggers

- How can you influence others to persuade you to do something you'd been planning to do anyway?
- How willing are you to be generous about sharing credit?
- Can you play down something you've done so that potential VLPS are encouraged to play it up?

Mischief Marketing Tip:

Find the unsung leader. No matter how large or small your ultimate target may be, always locate particular individuals having leverage over your target, and tailor your campaign to them.

Fuller Nabs VLP Ford

W̲hen cofounder Millard Fuller was building buzz for Habitat for Humanity, he already had Jimmy Carter and Rosalyn in his corner. In fact, he got the former president himself to swing a hammer here and there on behalf of Fuller's ingenious project to help poor people build their own homes. But Millard's mischief didn't stop there. He needed more VLPs.

By about 1986, what he needed was a conservative public supporter, someone who would complement Carter and send a signal to right-leaning folks that Habitat for Humanity was bipartisan. What he needed, in other words, was a Republican.

So he and his wife, Linda Fuller, made an appointment to meet with Gerald Ford at his home in Rancho Mirage, California. At that meeting, Millard jumped right in and asked Ford to serve on Habitat's board of advisors.

"Sure I'll serve on the advisory board," Ford told Fuller. "But I'm not a carpenter like Carter. Don't expect me to go around building houses." Thrilled to have another U.S. president, a

Mischief Marketing Plan Overview

With mischief marketing, you need to develop a marketing plan, just as you would for any other kind of marketing. In fact, mischief marketing is much like conventional marketing, except for the fact that it often takes the conventional concept of microtargeting to its logical limit.

Let's get a quick overview of how to construct a mischief marketing plan. Then we'll cover the phases of the plan in more detail.

Plan Phase 1: Creating Your Mission Statement

A mission statement is a vital part of any marketing campaign. It's an expression of who you are, and of what you're trying to do. When well-written, it can infuse life into your whole campaign.

A mission statement is much broader and more abstract—in short, much larger—than a simple statement of goals or a clever piece of ad copy. In some cases, it can be as large as a moose. So in this phase of your marketing plan, you'll construct a powerful mission statement that will guide you throughout your campaign.

Plan Phase 2: Setting Goals

In this phase of designing your plan, you will ask yourself, What am I trying to accomplish? And then you will answer that question—ideally through a megaphone in a public restroom. Do you want to market an idea? A product? A service? A business concept? A program to help end sexism, racism, ageism? Do you want to promote genuine freedom of speech? Shock the world with toenail clippers that actually work? Do you want to meet someone inaccessible? Is it the president? Actress Judi Dench?

Plan Phase 3: Setting Alternate Goals Using the Knight Fork Principle

What really distinguishes a set of mischief marketing goals from a set of conventional marketing goals is the knight fork principle.

In the game of chess, certain pieces (the knight and others) can threaten two or more of your opponent's pieces at the same time. Such a configuration is called a fork, and the most well-known type of fork is the knight fork. When you set up a situation like this, your opponent is *bound* to give you one of those threatened pieces. In other words, you're bound to win *something* on your next move, no matter what your opponent does.

Similarly, in mischief marketing, if you knight fork your goals properly, you are bound to achieve at least one of them *no matter what happens*.

Here is an example of knight forking:

A company invents a new kind of glue. Unfortunately, it doesn't stick very well. Goal A was not achieved. The company then takes that same glue, turns the situation around, and invents Post-It note pads—which suddenly have the *virtue* of not sticking very well (because now the notes are removable). In other words, a new objective is identified and achieved— instant knight fork. One way or another, the company wins.

If you were to plan this out in advance (which the inventors of Post-It did not) you would ask yourself:

Republican to boot, on his Habitat letterhead, Fuller reassured Ford that by just endorsing his ecumenical organization he would be rendering an important service. "No problem then," Ford replied. "I endorse Habitat."

Cleverly, Fuller had brought a small group of local journalists with him to Ford's office, including a leading television crew and a national magazine writer, who were all waiting outside for a post-meeting press conference. Somewhat surprised, Ford agreed to go out and say a few words, telling the reporters that because he "fully supported Habitat's good work," he had just "enthusiastically" agreed to join their board of advisers. "That single Ford statement opened the doors for other Republicans and conservatives to enter," Fuller recalled.

—Douglas Brinkley
The Unfinished Presidency: Jimmy Carter's Journey Beyond the White House
Viking, 1998

★ What can I do with my product or service if it works the way I want it to work?

★ What can I do with it if it doesn't work the way I want it to work?

★ What is the very least objective this campaign can achieve? For instance, can my family members and I get a few laughs out of this thing? Can we make some politician look ridiculous? Can we expose an injustice, or an instance of consumer fraud in banking? Can we get media attention for something worthwhile? Can we at least write a good article, or maybe just a cheap TV movie about our project—*no matter what happens?*

In conventional marketing, you usually whittle your goals down to just a few. You restrict your focus. In mischief marketing you do just the opposite. You always design several goals into your marketing plan—as many as possible.

Don't get me wrong: your offering may (and should) be simple, but your mischief marketing goals should be complex and multifaceted. I'll explain why (in Chapter 4), but first I have to send a copy of this book to Judi Dench, because getting to meet her is one of *my* alternate goals in writing it. That and getting my daughter to clean up her room.

Phase 4: Creating Your Unique Selling Proposition

Suppose your mischievous campaign works and you miraculously land an appointment with the very leveraged persons (VLPs) you targeted. Say your VLPs are Bill and Melinda Gates. You want their foundation to award your budding charity seventeen million dollars.

Now that you've got their attention, what are you going to say to them? After all, you need to say *something* intelligent about your offering, don't you? You can't just sit there at the meeting you worked so hard to get and start chortling inanely.

That's where your unique selling proposition (USP) comes in. Your USP is a statement of what makes you different from the competition. When FedEx got started, its USP had to do with guaranteeing to deliver packages overnight. That's what made it unique (at the time). No other company guaranteed overnight delivery.

What makes *you* different from everyone else? That's the question you need to answer when you craft your unique selling proposition in this phase.

Phase 5: Knowing What Can Go Wrong

What is likely to stop you from achieving your goals?

In conventional marketing, the biggest obstacles to achieving your goals are usually money, the nature of your competition, or possible changes in the market. The biggest blocks to effective mischief marketing are psychological, even spiritual, in nature.

You see, mischief marketing is much more involving, more demanding, more immersive, than conventional marketing. With mischief marketing, you can't just stare at a page of statistics and expect to extract from it a truly original idea for an advertising campaign ("Hey, I got it! Let's show the car atop a *mountain!*") It's like the difference between learning Japanese by reading a dictionary and learning by living and working right in the middle of Tokyo.

Because mischief marketing is so immersive—and because it's designed primarily for people who have no money or connections—it will engage you on a deep, personal level far more than any other kind of marketing. You'll put your heart and soul into it.

This process can be grueling, however, so you need to know how to deal with the psychological barriers you're likely to encounter. You need to be prepared for what can go wrong—mostly what can go wrong with how you will think and feel.

Phase 6: Identifying and Profiling Your VLP

In this phase, you'll decide what larger market you want to reach and determine which individuals (or small groups) are very leveraged persons in that market. Then you will research those VLPs with the thoroughness of a method actor to learn as much as you can about their personalities, speech habits, amours, wishes, families, friends, and foes.

Phase 7: Taking Stock of Your Tools

In this phase, you'll look at what basic resources are at your disposal as a mischief marketer. This depends partly on your finances, of course, but remember: many of the people featured in this book have done some amazing mischief marketing with very little money. So we'll focus on the cheapest tools you can use to your greatest advantage.

Phase 8: Scheduling

How much time are you willing to devote to a full-scale mischief marketing campaign? A month? A year?

Some campaigns take longer than others. If one of your objectives involves lunching with the Pope, for instance, your project could take years. And you might need to leverage your way through several jobs (such as president of the United States) before you manage to get there.

Phase 9: Timing Your Launch

In this phase, you'll plan how and when to launch your project and when to make specific tactical moves. Some simple examples of what we're talking about:

★ The best time to send mischievous E-mail is around 11:00 A.M. Pacific time (2:00 P.M. eastern)—not first thing in the morning.
★ The Christmas season is the worst time to launch a major campaign.

Phase 10: Budgeting

How much money are you willing to spend on a campaign? Better yet, how much *should* you spend? (Don't assume more is better; an overly expensive campaign could backfire, making you look like nothing more than a nut with money to burn.) In this phase, you'll sketch out your projected expenses in relation to your expected return on investment (ROI).

But your ROI might not be measured in dollars and cents at all. It might be incalculable, priceless. For instance, what would be the value to a writer—the ROI, if you will—of mischievously campaigning for and winning the Pulitzer Prize? Would it be the mere cash value of the prize? Of course not. It would be far greater than that.

Phase 11: Knowing the Rules

Knowing the rules—the mischief marketing commandments—that's what this phase of your marketing plan is about. Here is where you carefully review the legitimate boundaries of mischief marketing. Here is where you distinguish what you're doing from huckster marketing, scam marketing, hoax marketing—and every other sleazy variation. Here is where you draw the line between an authentic mischief marketing campaign and a crock of s**t.

Phase 12: Determining What Tactics to Use

In this phase you'll review some of the tactics mischief marketers use to get results and decide which ones apply to your situation. These tactics address the following issues:

★ How to get your foot in the door.
★ How to create credibility.
★ How to do a mischievous presentation.
★ How to use language in a special way that helps you establish a good relationship with your VLP.
★ How to fold advanced psychological sales techniques, which have been effective in conventional marketing for years, into your mischief marketing mix.

Phase 13: Inventing New Tactics by Studying Templative Tales

One mischief marketer made his small office seem busier than it really was by recording the background sounds of a truly busy office. Whenever anyone called, he'd flip on the recording and hold the phone near the speakers while he talked. Because customers thought he was busy, sales shot up.

Does that mean that you, too, should play a recording of a bustling office when you answer the phone? Of course not, especially if you run a funeral parlor. When you study a tale like this, ask yourself, "How can I *generalize* this tale? How can I extract the *essence* of what this person did? How can I apply it to my own situation?

So in this phase of your mischief marketing plan, you'll review the existing templative tales, start a collection of your own stories, list your favorites, and brainstorm about how to adapt them to your own unique situation.

Phase 14: Measuring Your Results

How do you know whether or not your campaign succeeded? How do you track which goals you've achieved and which are still outstanding? In this phase of your mischief marketing plan, you'll figure that out.

Phase 15: What If You Fail?

In this part of your marketing plan, you'll make sure that you have a backup plan in case your campaign goes wrong. More specifically, you'll figure out how to "judo" failure into opportunity.

Remember: in a well-designed mischief marketing campaign, you *always* win, you *always* achieve at least one of your goals. In fact, with mischief marketing, as with no other kind of marketing, your apparent failure to accomplish something often lays the foundation for your overall success at achieving your objectives. The rock that most people toss away becomes your cornerstone.

Example: suppose you decide you want to meet the CEO of General Motors, and suppose your campaign succeeds. You do meet the guy, but he isn't receptive to your message or your offering. In fact, he's somewhat rude to you.

Did your campaign fail at the goal of meeting the VLP? No, it succeeded at that. Did it fail at the goal of getting him to act on your message? Yes. But can you judo that failure and turn the whole situation around? Of course.

In fact, that is exactly what mischievous filmmaker Michael Moore did when he made the hilarious movie *Roger & Me* (his first film). On the surface, *Roger & Me* is all about Michael's failure to market a certain message to a certain VLP. But ultimately, of course, it's about his success at marketing that same message to the rest of the world.

Mischievous Pop Quiz

1. You study mischief marketing tales in order to:
   a) copycat them.
   b) adapt the essence of each tale to your unique situation.
   c) learn from their mistakes.

2. If your target is a large company, you should:
   a) communicate with the human resources department.
   b) hire a primatologist to communicate with the human resources department using sign language and a large number of bananas.
   c) find a well-leveraged person in the company and communicate with her or him.

3. Knight forking means:
   a) engaging in sexual activity with medieval men-at-arms.
   b) devising alternative goals so that, no matter what happens, you always achieve at least one of them.
   c) getting your daughter to clean up her room.

YOUR MISSION STATEMENT

Ah, life.

In this life, we all tend to get caught up in the details of whatever we happen to be doing (no matter what it is) to the point where we can't see the forest for the trees. This is true about everything, not just marketing.

Here's an example. A friend of yours—and we all know someone like this—wants to tell you about a great movie he just saw. He wants to persuade you to see it, too. In a sense, he wants to "sell" you on seeing that movie, but he goes about it like this:

"Oh, boy. I saw this great movie a few weeks ago. You gotta see it. It takes place in Boston . . . no, wait. It takes place in New York. Wait. No, that's right. Boston. And it stars that guy. Who's that actor—the one with the hair? You know who I mean. He's in all those horror movies. Who am I thinking of? He used to be married to what's-her-name, the blonde. C'mon! What's his name? You know the guy I'm talking about, right? He's so funny!"

What happened to your friend? He's gotten lost in small details about what he wants to communicate to you, instead of getting to the essence of it.

Well, the same thing happens in business. You may *think* you're selling Volvos, but you're really in the business of selling safety and reliability. If you start blabbing on about the engine, the tires, and whatnot, you'll never get a chance to discuss what your customer really wants to hear about—namely, safety and reliability.

Your mission statement is what will keep you on track when you start getting lost in details, trundling off the deep end, and losing track of what business you're really in. It will prevent your from getting MAD—marketing Alzheimer's disease.

Of the many literary traps into which a writer may fall, the insertion of an irrelevant, indecipherable, and ungrammatical quotation that ends abruptly, foolishly.

—UTA ELLISATT

There are differences between a mission statement in conventional marketing and a mission statement in mischief marketing. The table here summarizes some of these differences:

	Conventional Marketing	Mischief Marketing
Term	Mission Statement	Mischievous Mission Statement
Definition	A short text that makes explicit what business you're really in.	A short text that makes explicit what you are trying to accomplish in life, not just in business.
Scenario	You're a graphic artist. You may think you're in the business of drawing and painting, but you're really in the business of communicating. Your mission statement would therefore reflect this.	You're producing a TV show about gardening. You may think you're in the business of talking about gardening, but you're really in the business of helping people enjoy and appreciate life without spending a lot of money.
Example	"Our mission: To communicate."	"Our mission: To help people experience life's simpler pleasures."

Here are some important points to keep in mind when you create your mission statement:

★ A mission statement should express who you are, what you do, what you believe in, and why you believe in it.
★ Don't confuse a mission statement with a slogan, business plan, goal, advertising piece, public relations piece, or world peace.
★ Some of the most powerful mission statements are only a few sentences long.
★ Look at other mission statements to get ideas about how to approach your own. Keep it simple.
★ To develop a truly vigorous mission statement, take your time.

★ In your statement, avoid bragging about how swell you are, or about what matchless quality and great service you provide. Everybody says these things.

★ Honesty, simplicity, frankness are good components of a mission statement.

★ Eloquent, grandiose statements don't have much impact. The best statements are direct and powerful. For example: "Mission statement: To let my kids know that they don't need to be afraid to pursue their dreams."

★ Make sure your statement reflects you, and not some other company or person. Even if your statement is a bit awkward—in fact, especially if it's a bit awkward—it will ring truer than it would if you tried to look like something you're not.

★ Believe in your statement. If you don't believe in it, neither will anyone else. Everyone you meet will know you're just full of it.

★ Don't use your mission statement all by itself. Instead, use it as an integral part of your entire campaign.

★ Review and edit your statement at least once every two months. It will help you stay on track.

★ A good mission statement should tell your story in less than thirty seconds because most people have a short attention span.

It was for a good reason that the marketing community borrowed the word "mission" from the field of evangelism. In evangelism and theology, the word is very powerful. It carries what psychologist Carl Jung called numinosity. "Mission" is more than a word; it is almost a symbol that glows (becomes numinous) in your imagination. It's a kind of place holder for your vision.

Sleepless Man on a Mission Inspires His Kids

*F*or many years, Jeff Arch struggled to be a successful writer. Things were difficult for so long that he eventually gave up and did something else. Then, after his son was born in 1989, Arch decided to start writing again.

Quoted below on the subject of what motivated him to try again (that is, on the subject of his mission, as he saw it) is the author of the screenplay for the enormous hit *Sleepless in Seattle*:

"I got serious," Arch said. "I was proud of what I was doing, but I found I was starting to spin my wheels. I realized every single time I put my mind to something, no matter what it was, I got it. I got it fairly and pretty much on my terms."

So he made his mind up he wanted to write a hit film. "I thought, 'What can I tell my children about their dreams if I don't go after mine?' The idea of being a fraud by my own children just drove me crazy. I couldn't handle it. They deserved this."

—SUSAN KING
"Sweet Dreams for 'Sleepless' Writer"
Los Angeles Times,
June 29, 1993

Your Constitution, Should You Decide to Accept It

Your mission statement describes what you're really about. And if you're a publisher or a reporter, what you're often really about is not just manufacturing sound bites, but also defending the First Amendment to the Constitution.

Random House founder Bennett Cerf often took a mischievous tack when it came to marketing his new publishing company and fulfilling his First Amendment mission at the same time. After he met James Joyce, whose *Ulysses* had been banned for obscenity in the United States, Cerf sued the government on Joyce's behalf. To spark publicity for the lawsuit (and the book) Cerf persuaded an envoy to bring a copy of *Ulysses* from Europe through U.S. customs—and to insist that the customs agent search the bags and confiscate the book. The agent obliged. And so, amid a flurry of bureaucratic fuss, Cerf's legal show hit the road right on schedule.

What few knew was that, inside the book, Cerf had craftily pasted reviews hailing *Ulysses* as a great work

If you can craft a mission statement that deeply reflects who you are and what you and your company are up to, it will carry you over the rough spots of your daily grind and reunite you with your vision.

The Real Mission of *Mischief Marketing*

Here's the actual mission statement for this book:

Mischief Marketing is designed (a) to find its way, some lonely night, into the hands of one particular reader who has a significant business-related mission to fulfill in life but who's currently too young; too old; too poor; too marginalized; too burdened with depression, illness, addiction, or pain; too contemptuous of our greed-based culture; or just too tired to get started on the path to the fulfillment of that mission. And (b) to provide that person with the marketing tools he or she needs to stop making excuses and please get started already.

For more on mission statements, check out mischiefmarketing.com.

Setting Goals and Alternative (Knight Fork) Goals

Setting Goals

Once you have your mission statement, you can start setting goals. But again, there's a difference between setting goals in conventional marketing, and setting goals in mischief marketing.

In conventional marketing, most of your goals will be obvious, and they will usually be financial. They'll tend to look like this:

★ Increase revenue 75 percent by this time next year.
★ Reach the Generation Y market without appearing to be selling anything.
★ Change the perception of your business.

In mischief marketing, your goals will tend to look more like this:

★ Have a blast.
★ Make disadvantaged people aware of the fact that, if they don't get involved in politics and marketing very soon, their situation will only get worse.
★ Meet some rich celebrity at a rehab facility and marry him or her.
★ Make and market a film, as the directors of *The Blair Witch Project* did.
★ Convey important social or moral concepts, as Martin Luther King or Mother Teresa did.
★ Reach a market considered impossible to penetrate, as Estée Lauder did.
★ Market some truly important ideas by appearing to market trivial nonsense. (Animators and cartoonists do this all the time, by the way.)
★ Encourage your kids to do their homework.

Please sit down with me here for a moment while I elaborate on that last one. I know it looks out of place. How can mischief marketing help you encourage your kids to do their homework? Isn't mischief marketing primarily about business, about selling things?

Yes and no. Mischief marketing is as much about selling ideas and values as it is about business. In fact, discussing business is just the vehicle—the Trojan Horse, if you will—that makes it possible for you to be reading this book in the first place.

of literature. In those days, such reviews would not normally have been admissible as evidence. But because they were literally pasted into the contraband volume, they went along with it for the ride to court and slipped into evidence.

The company won the highly publicized lawsuit, *Ulysses* became a bestseller, and Random House found itself well on its way from quirky upstart to major player (and champion of free speech).

—Adapted from JOHN TEBBEL's *History of Book Publishing in the United States*, as cited by ANNA BRAY DUFF in *Investor's Business Daily*, March 17, 1999

Idea Joggers

- What can you do to enlarge your mission so that it concerns something greater than simply whether or not you'll make a ton of money?
- Are you passionate about the emergence of a new form of capitalism, for example? Then how can you incorporate that larger vision into your mission?
- Before you even think about mischief marketing, ask yourself, What genuinely inspires me? What makes me feel as though my life has meaning?

W riter Mark Dery and artist Joey Skaggs are among the proponents of a mischievous and potentially useful and educational activity called "culture jamming."

Culture jammers point out that our behavior—and even the way we think—is controlled by the mass media (especially advertisers and marketers). Of course, we can't detect the hype/nosis they foist on us any more than a fish can detect the presence of water, but it's there, and we swim in it.

Culture jamming, therefore, is about using mischievous techniques to expose how giant corporations puppeteer us. It's about ripping open the curtain to expose the frail, old man behind the smoke and mirrors, as Toto did in that famous movie.

Is there a way out of . . . the society of the spectacle? Yes. You can take charge of your mental environment, and become a culture jammer. Culture jamming means semiotic jujitsu—using media power against itself. The Adbusters' Media Foundation does this all the time with famous spoofs of the Absolut Vodka ads ("Absolut death," etc.). Other culture jammers often take commercials or TV programs and replace the

The moral flabbiness born of the exclusive worship of the bitch-goddess Success. That—with the squalid cash interpretation put on the word success—is our national disease.

—WILLIAM JAMES
The Letters of William James, vol. 2
Atlantic Monthly Press, 1920

The language of the marketplace has eclipsed all other forms of rhetoric. Don't worry, they're saying, we're not going to ask you to even think of community and civic responsibility or any-thing that is not in your direct, economic self-interest—and, somehow, a nation that we can be proud of will materialize.

—CONSERVATIVE
COLUMNIST ARIANNA
HUFFINGTON
salon.com
September 16, 1999

Here are some ideas for marketing the value of homework to your kids.

☛ Do your kids admire a particular celebrity? Then launch a mischievous letter-writing campaign to persuade that celebrity to call your kids up and encourage them to do their homework. No, I'm *not* kidding. Do you realize that one phone call or one short letter from someone like Michael Jordan can turn a kid's life around in a matter of minutes? Of course you do.

☛ Do your kids admire a particular kind of music? Then encourage them to learn something about how that music is made. Target a campaign to the chief engineer at a major recording studio, and make it your goal to persuade him or her to let your kids sit in on a recording or editing session. Let your kids see for themselves that far more transpires behind the scenes than they might have imagined. Maybe that revelation will interest them in some other aspect of the music business. If your campaign works, your kids will also realize that you can't operate sound editing or video equipment very well if you can't read.

In short, take advantage of the worship of fame that dominates our culture. Craft mischief marketing campaigns that will help put our society's grossly overpaid celebrities to work on helping your kids. Aren't your kids worth the effort of a concerted mischief marketing campaign that points them in the right direction in life? Or would you rather waste time hollering at them and putting up a front about how concerned you are? With your kids or with any of your prospects, turn the machinery of the mass media culture to your own advantage.

In the culture jamming example, Mizrach is talking about parodying our media-crazed culture, but that isn't the only way to do culture jamming.

When you're designing your mischief marketing goals, ask yourself:

★ How can my product or service educate people about how they're being manipulated, especially by my competitors?

★ How can I get the U.S. attorney general to make my kids do their homework?

dialogue and soundtrack with something subversive. Yet others take to billboards or road signs and cleverly rearrange the letters to say something different. As one activist suggests, "Where critique is no longer a possibility, parody is always an alternative response."

—STEVE MIZRACH
"Culture Jamming: Information War of the 90's"
Mediacy, Fall 1995

Simple Goals

Sometimes, your mischief marketing goals may be very simple.

In fact, you could say that, back in 1964, musician Reg Dwight's goal was simply to put himself in the same room as his VLPS— nothing more. Of course, that room happened to be a recording studio, and Dwight's job as a messenger for Mills Music eventually led to the publication of his first song.

About two years later, Reg once again got after-hours access to a different studio. This time, however, he met studio owner Dick James, who promptly took on the job of nurturing his solo career.

(continued)

By the way, Reg Dwight at one point changed his name—to Elton John.

So you see, your goals don't need to be terribly ambitious or complicated.

Monitoring the Side Effects of Your Goals

You often need to carefully consider, not only your goals, but their possible side effects as well. This is especially true in mischief marketing, which can actually be dangerous, as the following tale shows.

In the 1930s, before television, families gathered around the radio for entertainment every night after dinner. On the eve of Halloween in 1938, this harmless activity caused mass panic. That was the night Orson Welles ran "War of the Worlds," a series of "news bulletins" apparently interrupting a normal musical show.

Now Welles's goal was to provide some mischievous amusement on Halloween, and his highly realistic "news coverage" of martians invading the earth did in fact include several disclaimers that made it clear the whole event was noth-

These are the kinds of questions you need to ask yourself before you sit down in earnest to design your mischief marketing goals.

No matter how many goals you may have, there will usually be one overriding goal common to every mischief marketing campaign: to appear larger or more well known than you are at the moment. The following table summarizes the important differences between conventional and mischief marketing goals.

Setting Goals	
In Conventional Marketing	**In Mischief Marketing**
Narrow your focus. Set only a few goals.	Broaden your focus. Set many goals.
Keep your goals centered on bottom-line business factors (money).	Extend your goals to incorporate personal, family-related, and spiritual factors.
Think like a military commander who pinpoints one or two specific targets.	Think like a military commander who carpet bombs as many targets as possible, knowing she's bound to hit something eventually.
Set reasonable, achievable goals. Aim for the wood, not the chopping block.	Set unreasonable, impossible goals. Aim for the chopping block, not the wood.
Design sensible goals that have a useful purpose.	Design absurd goals that have no purpose other than to amuse you and your friends.
Stop kidding around.	Yeah, right.

Defining Your Unique Selling Proposition

Even though your mischief marketing campaign may (and should) have many goals, your core

offering should be very simple and focused because you don't want to confuse people. Ideally, it should be just one, unique thing.

Case in point: when Xerox first tried to make personal computers, it didn't sell many of them because the brand name confused people. To most customers, who have one-track minds, Xerox meant copy machines and nothing else.

Examples of unique core offerings include:

★ a book called *The Interpretation of Dreams*
★ the Civil Rights Act of 1964
★ slot machines whose proceeds go to good causes

Now we come to your unique selling proposition (USP). It's what distinguishes you from the competition. For example, if you're writing a business book, you might want to distinguish your book from other, similar books, by introducing new acronyms or terms, as authors Al Ries and Jack Trout did in their excellent book, *Positioning*. The concept not only provided the USP for the book, but it also introduced a genuinely useful thinking tool.

Your unique selling proposition is what you're going to bring to the table when your mischief marketing finally succeeds in reaching your prospect. When you finally meet with your VLP, your mischief marketing campaign becomes like the first stage of a rocket—something that drops away, no longer needed.

Suppose you plan to launch a charity organization that's based on a game in which you buy and sell "play shares" of stock whose prices are strictly tied to their real-world counterparts but are fractionally lower. Commission or membership fees go to the charity. The whole game is supervised by authorities in securities, gaming, and philanthropy (which is why you'd need a lot of money—to pay the lawyers who'll design the legal infrastructure). Stock trading games already exist, of course, but most of them

ing more than a radio drama. But the side effect of his talent for realism was awful. Many Americans missed the disclaimers, or didn't understand them, and believed we were being invaded. The streets jammed with the cars of terrified people fleeing their homes.

The next time Welles did something mischievous, you can bet he paid attention to the potential side effects of his goals.

Who Was That Masked Man?

*J*eremy Barbera started Metro Services Group with only $900 in personal seed money. Working from his living room, here are some of the mischievous things Jeremy did to meet his goal of landing big, important clients like American Express:

• Through a business incubator, he rented an address on prestigious Madison Avenue.
• On an average day, after phoning a client to discuss a proposal, he'd promise that his "secretary" would type it up immediately and that he'd send the proposal to the client "via messenger."

(continued)

- Barbera was both the secretary and the messenger. After he hung up the phone, he'd type up the proposal, change into his sweatpants, jump on his bike, and deliver the proposal.

As Barbara puts it:

"I was CEO at 2 P.M., secretary at 3:30 P.M., and messenger at 4:30 P.M."

Barbera says he lived in fear—well merited, as it turned out—of discovery. As bike messenger he had befriended a client's security guard. When Barbera subsequently appeared downtown to meet with that client (this time in CEO mode), he encountered the guard. She buzzed upstairs and announced, "Metro's messenger is down here, and he claims he has a meeting with you." Thinking quickly, Barbera responded to his customer's confusion, "Oh, my brother used to work for me delivering packages when he was down on his luck." Barbera sustained this multi-role juggling for two years.

—C. CAGGIANO
"Bootstrapping: Great Companies Started with $1,000 or Less"
Inc., August 1995

By 1994, Barbera's company had made $6.4 million in revenue. Would you say he achieved at least some of his financial goals using mischief marketing tactics?

don't benefit charity. So your unique selling proposition to Bill and Melinda would point out that yours is the only game devoted to charity (or the only one devoted to a particular charity). This would be the USP of your offering.

Case in point: the USP for *Mischief Marketing* is "Marketing for people who hate marketing." Since no other marketing book specifically addresses the needs of people who despise marketing, *Mischief Marketing* is unique among such books.

Mischievous Pop Quiz

1. **You should write a mission statement because:**
   a) I said so.
   b) it will help you define what business you're really in.
   c) it will give you something to do while you're downloading a big file.

2. **A good mission statement should be short because:**
   a) people these days have a short attention span.

PROFILING YOUR VLP

Conventional Research Techniques

In the research phase of your campaign, you find out as much as you can about your prospect so you can tailor your efforts to that person or tightly focused group.

There are at least two kinds of research techniques you can use to help you learn about your VLPs, their businesses, and their interests: conventional, and mischievous.

All kinds of books have been written about conventional approaches to research, but you'll save yourself a lot of time and energy if you remember this one basic tactic: get a librarian to help you find out whatever you need to know about your prospect.

Ah, librarians. Those quiet, humble people, often with thick, funny glasses, who guard over the public treasures of knowledge. What do you think about them? C'mon, tell the truth. Don't you secretly think they're just wimps who couldn't find work in that enormous pissing contest we call corporate America?

Well, if you think that, you're wrong.

Librarians are among the most amazing knowledge detectives you will ever encounter. You wouldn't know it to look at them, but these people are truly hunters—hunters of data. Equal in tracking skill to any tribal leader in any jungle, librarians can ferret out just about any info-quarry imaginable. Picture them half-naked, with lithe bodies and painted faces, spearing pages out of books left and right. That's what they'd look like if they weren't wearing their wimp camouflage.

The Power of Research

Mostly as a labor of love, Oprah Winfrey did an extraordinary amount of research on *The Color Purple* before auditioning for a role in the film. In fact, she virtually memorized the entire book. When she read for Steven Spielberg, her understanding of the material was so deep that she got the part even though she wasn't a professional actress at the time. Diligent research can produce powerful results. In this case, it propelled Winfrey onto the national scene and prepared the way for her illustrious career.

Luckily, most people don't know this about librarians. They fall for the wimp camouflage and end up wasting time hunting down information on their own. Why run around wondering where you can get information about your VLP when you can simply ask a librarian to help you?

Whether you get a librarian to help you or decide to conduct your own research, here are some questions you should be able to answer about your prospect:

In terms of personal matters, you'll want to know:

★ What are your VLP's hobbies and outside interests?
★ How many kids does your VLP have? What are their ages?
★ What is his or her spouse like?
★ What is your VLP's ethnic background? What sort of a family does he or she come from?
★ What customs prevail in that ethnic group? What kind of jokes? What modes of expression?
★ What part of the country does your VLP come from? What are the customs and mannerisms in that region?
★ What's your VLP's favorite food?
★ Does your VLP favor a certain lingo? How does he or she talk and write?

On the business front, you'll want to know:

★ How is your VLP's business doing?
★ What are its revenues this year? What were they last year?
★ What about profitability? What about margins?
★ How many people does the business employ?
★ How do employees feel about the work atmosphere there?

★ What do financial analysts have to say about the business?
★ Who are your prospect's competitors?
★ What do the competitors' financials look like?

You can find this type of information in the following sources:

★ *Hoover's Handbook*
★ *Wall Street Journal* Briefing Books
★ *Contemporary Authors* (if your VLP has written any books)
★ *Who's Who*
★ InfoTrac (for newspaper and magazine articles)
★ Books on investigating people. Follow the instructions.

Internet sources might include:

★ search engines
★ usenet groups (investor groups, etc)
★ searchable databases
★ Lexis-Nexis (for just about everything imaginable—if you can get an account with a school or law firm)
★ genealogical information. They may have inherited or otherwise picked up a love of ragtime or gardening from grandpa.

For more information on this kind of research, visit mischief marketing.com.

Mischievous Info Gathering: Birth-Order Theory

Now we come to the mischievous profiling techniques.

Birth-order theory provides you, the mischief marketer, with a surprisingly effective tool for understanding your prospect. It is less like an x-ray machine and more like a compass. In other words, it can't reveal a lot of hidden things, but it can guide you toward discovering something valuable about your prospect's personality.

What is birth-order theory? In a nutshell, it has to do with whether you were born into your family earlier or later than your brothers and sisters. Many researchers believe that when you appeared chronologically in your family can have a significant impact on your personality. Of course, other factors such as heredity and environment also play a big part. Nevertheless, because some studies suggest that our position in the family inclines us toward developing certain emotional responses, behavior patterns, and ways of thinking about the world, birth-order research can help you harvest clues about your prospect's personality. It can tell you what to expect of your prospect, what to avoid, and how to elicit the responses you want. Before we explore the characteristics of people in terms of this theory, please keep in mind two things. The first is that wherever I assert, for example, that "X is true," I usually mean that X is *probably* true, based on current research about birth-order theory. (I figured you would probably get tired of my using the word "probably" all the time.) The second point is that I haven't the faintest idea to what extent this birth-order stuff is true. It seems to be true of many people, but it may apply only to some.

Firstborns and Earlyborns

Firstborns and earlyborns are highly motivated to achieve. Most astronauts, for example, were either firstborns or onlyborns (only children). And there are a high percentage of firstborns among U.S. presidents.

In school, your firstborn prospects worked hard to get good grades, and they still work hard. In fact, they are intensely competitive. They are also perfectionists, so you're not going to slip any little details past them. Because their parents expected a lot from them when they were young, they tend to do things faster than other people and to approach life more seriously. They like to follow the rules and set an example for others. They can be pretty bossy.

In summary, firstborns (and earlyborns):

★ like to set goals
★ are responsible
★ stick to the rules
★ are organized
★ are grounded
★ are determined

Implications for Mischief Marketing

In light of these characteristics, if you're targeting a firstborn prospect, you'll want your offering—no matter how wacky it is—to appear somehow conservative, or at least disciplined in conception and execution.

For instance, suppose you're offering an entirely new kind of service to a firstborn prospect. Take something really wild—like on-demand child care, where you can actually take your kids someplace trustworthy for just two hours, instead of having to sign them up for six months in advance. In that case, you'll want to emphasize not how different your service is, but how similar it is to other services that already have a track record. For instance, you'll want to say something like, "This is nothing more than Chuck E Cheese's, but with trained baby-sitters and video monitors."

In other words, your initial marketing foray (that is, what you do to contact your prospect and get an appointment) might be wacky and mischievous, sure. Why not? But your *follow-up* to a firstborn should be more level-headed. You should have a complete (nonmischievous) business plan, with all your numbers carefully worked out and all objections or contingencies addressed.

Following are a few more tips for dealing with firstborns:

★ Keep wacky humor to a minimum.
★ Maintain a conservative exterior (within the bounds of your mischievousness).
★ Demonstrate that you put a lot of good, hard work into your campaign and your offering.
★ Pay strict attention to the smallest details.
★ Do not emphasize how different your offering is. Instead, highlight how similar it is to something else that everyone understands.
★ Do not suddenly leap onto a conference table in the middle of your presentation and start shrieking, "How is it possible that on-demand, short-term child care does not yet exist except in a few malls? Why is it that nearly all current child care services require long-term commitments?"
★ With a firstborn prospect, what you should do instead is leap onto a *chair*; then start shrieking.

Onlyborns

Only children are in a category of their own. They are self-confident, and have what amounts to a mission, or calling, in life. In other words, they have a sense of responsibility to the world. Onlyborns don't need to compete with others in order to do their best. They are natural-born leaders.

Implications for Mischief Marketing

If you're targeting onlyborn prospects, almost anything goes. There's no telling what onlyborns will do, or what sort of campaign or offering they'll respond to. There are no rules here. Sorry!

Laterborns

Laterborns are good mediators who know how to get along with others. Laterborn kids don't have their parents all to themselves, so they learn to compromise and negotiate. Your prospect is probably an excellent manager and leader.

Laterborns—especially lastborns (youngest kids)—have a great sense of humor, and it's eclectic. They understand and enjoy slapstick, irony, wry wit, tragicomedy, zany humor, raucous humor, visual humor, musical humor—you name it. Where most people respond only to one or two types of humor, laterborns and lastborns respond to anything that's funny (even to things earlyborns would shake their heads at and call kid's stuff). To a mischief marketer, to know something about a person's sense of humor is to know something valuable indeed.

In summary, laterborns are:

★ creative
★ good diplomats
★ sociable
★ generous
★ flexible
★ not shy about challenging authority
★ gifted at motivating others
★ not risk-averse

Implications for Mischief Marketing

If you're targeting laterborn prospects, you have a lot of latitude in terms of how you can design your campaign. It's okay to be a little weird or flamboyant; your laterborn prospects won't mind. In fact, they might even like it. And, of course, you should use humor liberally. Pull out all the stops.

Before you act upon your birth-order research, remember that birth-order theory isn't a simplistic system. It doesn't say that all firstborns, or all lastborns, are precisely like this or that. These are just general characteristics. Dynamics within the family can alter these influences, and many variables can affect a family. These include: gender, the number of years between children, physical differences or disabilities, the birth-order positions of the parents, influences that arise from blending families following divorce or death, and the relationship between the parents.

For details on birth-order theory, see mischiefmarketing.com.

Mischievous Info Gathering: Astrology

Believe it or not, there seems to be a certain amount of truth to the ancient study of astrology. In fact, a number of respected scientists are now beginning to explore the potential of astrology and are trying to devise ways to use its insights. In this section I will discuss how you, too, can use astrology in the privacy of your own home to perhaps gain some insight into your prospects.

I will now pause while half the readers slam down the book and leave in a huff. Thank you for coming. Good-bye. The rest of these remarks are for those who remain. But because even open-minded people sometimes need a little nudge, let's first review quickly what I am not saying here.

☛ I am not saying that astrology is completely valid. I am saying only that it is worth a second look, and that you might find it helpful—in your mischief marketing. In fact, what I'm really saying is that astrology, apart from the question of its scientific validity, can help you tap unconscious resources that enrich creativity.

☛ I am not talking about the kind of astrology you see in the newspapers. That kind of astrology—which is based on your sun sign—is almost always bogus.

☛ I am not going to address certain highly technical issues raised by scientific studies like those conducted by the Gauquelins, for example, or by Carlson, Glickman, Rawlings, Culver and Ianna, or anyone else. For details on formal scientific studies, critiques, and defenses of astrology, please visit www.mischiefmarketing.com.

On the other hand, I am going to mention a few interesting tidbits about astrology. They all have a bearing on the application of astrology to business—specifically the business of mischief marketing.

Some of the greatest scientists in history thought astrology had validity. Some of them (Johannes Kepler, for example) actually were professional astrologers, at least part time. A number of Wall Street traders use astrology, and so did the Reagan White House. Yet many skeptics hate astrology as much as the Catholic Church once hated Darwin.

Some years ago, a group of prominent scientists and Nobel Prize winners approached the brilliant skeptic and popular astronomer Carl Sagan

> *I was born at 17:58 Greenwich mean time on December 28, 1944, in Lenoir, North Carolina. You can find out more about me from that than you can from reading this book.*
>
> —BIOCHEMIST KARY MULLIS
> *Dancing Naked in the Mine Fields*
> Pantheon Books, 1998

to sign a proclamation condemning astrology. He refused because he thought the condemnation was too dogmatic in tone—in other words, it was unscientific. This refusal cost Sagan a few friends.

You need to tap the deep, creative resources of your unconscious mind in order to conceive and execute successful mischief marketing campaigns. Astrology represents an ancient tradition that probably (repeat: probably) goes back to Stonehenge and beyond. As such, its symbols and ideas form part of our collective unconscious and are very powerful. Therefore, like great poetry and religious iconography, the symbols and ideas of astrology are capable of eliciting deep responses from your unconscious mind. In other words, the symbols of astrology can help you tap your own creative resources. This effect is independent of the scientific validity of astrology.

Here's another way to put this argument: I can't prove scientifically that my family is the greatest family in the world, but I feel it is. This feeling inspires me to do many things, some of which have provable validity. But without my family, I could not do these provable things. So my ability to do something scientifically provable is based on something scientifically unprovable. Something similar is true for astrology. You can use unproved or unprovable information from astrology to arrive at provable information about your prospect.

The main points are that astrology does seem to have some validity and that it can help you understand your prospects.

Many studies of astrology have lacked real control groups. Although researchers asked a group of astrologers to match natal charts with personality profiles, they never asked a parallel (control) group of psychologists to match *their* measuring instruments (like the Minnesota Multiphasic Personality Inventory, for example) with similar profiles. Moreover, virtually every study done on astrology to date has assumed that it is legitimate to select your subjects randomly. This is like trying to prove that the earth has (or does not have) a gravitational field by observing the behavior of randomly selected objects from all over the known universe instead of restricting your selection to objects near the earth.

In other words, it may be that the people for whom astrology really works are those who voluntarily wander into its "orbit" rather than those whose names were plucked out of the phone book by research assistants.

In real astrology, not the newspaper kind, your sun sign is only one factor in your natal chart (the map of the heavens at the moment of your birth). The factors in astrology that really count are the houses and the planets, so it's a good idea to discover which planets are most prominent in your prospect's chart.

You may need to ask a professional astrologer to help you, or you may need to study enough about astrology to figure it out yourself, but it will be well worth your while to do so.

Following is a summary of so-called planetary characteristics with a mischief marketing spin.

Solar Prospects

Prospects with a prominent Sun are likely to be:

★ confident
★ abundant in vitality
★ outgoing, spontaneous
★ leaders
★ optimistic
★ not easily swayed by the opinions of others
★ sometimes overbearing

Recommendations for Mischief Marketing Communications

★ Use a friendly tone.
★ Project confidence, but avoid brashness or gushing.

Recommendations for Types of Humor

★ Use storytelling formats. Example: "A rabbi, a nun, and an Irishman walk into a bar in New York City. the bartender takes one look at them and says, 'What is this? A joke?'"
★ Avoid highly verbal or subtle humor, but don't be crude, either.
★ Use silly humor sparingly. Example: the scene in *Monty Python and the Holy Grail* in which John Cleese and his traveling companions encounter some people who identify themselves by declaring shrilly, "We . . . are The Knights . . . Who Say . . . 'Ni!'"

Lunar Prospects

Prospects with a prominent Moon are likely to be:

★ hypersensitive
★ quick to adapt to new situations
★ restless
★ indecisive
★ moody
★ procrastinating
★ protective
★ nurturing

Recommendations for Mischief Marketing Communications

★ Be persistent. Lunar prospects don't trust anyone at first.
★ Research your prospect's pet peeves. If you share any, let your prospect know.
★ If you surprise your lunar prospect with a mischievous campaign, be sure to apologize for the mischievousness at some point.

Recommendations for Types of Humor

★ Use dark humor—the humor of suffering, of the oppressed. Think Woody Allen.
★ Try humor that reveals a deep understanding of people.
★ Use silly humor sparingly, or flag it as silly before you use it. Give warning.

Mercurial Prospects

Prospects with a prominent Mercury are likely to be:

★ quick-witted
★ well-read and literate
★ good communicators
★ good writers
★ scattered
★ glib, witty

Recommendations for Mischief Marketing Communications

★ Be meticulous in terms of grammar, spelling, and syntax.
★ Keep your tone light and breezy.

★ Avoid anything that may seem scholarly or pedantic, but be meticulous about your information sources.

Recommendations for Types of Humor

★ Try for wry, ironic, or generally verbal (as opposed to crude or slapstick) humor.
★ Silly humor is perfectly okay with mercurial prospects.
★ Use Steven Wright's type of humor.

I went to a general store. They wouldn't let me buy anything specifically.

—STEVEN WRIGHT

Venusian Prospects

Prospects with a prominent Venus are likely to be:

★ artistic
★ kind and gentle
★ diplomatic
★ sensual
★ charming
★ deeply dedicated to family and friends
★ gifted with a sense of humor

Recommendations for Mischief Marketing Communications

★ Emphasize the physical beauty of your communications. Use the most gorgeous paper you can find, the finest envelopes or wrapping paper. Spend a lot of time choosing fonts and colors. If possible, hire a professional graphic designer to create your packages.
★ Use a gentle, steady voice. Avoid sounding like Fran Drescher.
★ Stay light.

Recommendations for Types of Humor

★ Use conventional humor; nothing too wild.
★ Use mildly racy sexual humor.
★ Some silliness is okay, but not too much.

Martian Prospects

Prospects with a prominent Mars are likely to be:

★ highly energetic
★ somewhat opinionated
★ workaholics
★ ambitious
★ aggressive, or at least assertive
★ practical, pragmatic

Recommendations for Mischief Marketing Communications

★ Emphasize the practicality of your offering.
★ Make your letters or phone calls short and to the point.
★ Keep everything upbeat and energetic. Think Tony Robbins.
★ Borrow a set of teeth from a horse.

Recommendations for Types of Humor

★ Go for bawdy humor.
★ Cutting humor and sarcasm work well.
★ Avoid silliness.

Jupiterian Prospects

Prospects with a prominent Jupiter are likely to be:

★ broad-minded
★ optimistic
★ trustworthy
★ benevolent
★ sometimes fat
★ in possession of strong moral or religious convictions
★ in possession of felony convictions. No, just kidding.
★ good leaders, educators

Recommendations for Mischief Marketing Communications

★ Emphasize how helpful your offering could be to disadvantaged people.
★ If your offering has an educational aspect, highlight it.

Recommendations for Types of Humor

★ Almost any kind of humor will entertain prospects with a prominent Jupiter.

Saturnian Prospects

Prospects with a prominent Saturn are likely to be:

★ conservative
★ serious, determined
★ a little stiff
★ highly self-disciplined
★ prone to depression
★ not thrilled with the concept of mischief marketing

Recommendations for Mischief Marketing Communications

★ Emphasize the serious side of your offering.
★ Explain that you used a mischievous technique only because you had no choice, and that your offering was too important to await a more conservative treatment.
★ If your initial mischievous approach worked, keep all subsequent communications formal and nonmischievous.

Recommendations for Types of Humor

★ Try for the humor of Dr. Kevorkian.
★ Use grim, heavy-handed goofiness; in other words, silly humor gone wrong.
★ In general, with a saturnine prospect, you would have better luck trying to make a cat laugh.

Uranian Prospects

Prospects with a prominent Uranus are likely to be:

★ eccentric
★ inventive, trailblazing
★ somewhat crazy
★ obsessed with independence and freedom
★ afflicted with OCD (obsessive-compulsive disorder)
★ willful
★ impulsive
★ open-minded
★ handicapped by an inability to relax

Recommendations for Mischief Marketing Communications

★ Emphasize the unusual or unique character of your offering.
★ Go all out with your mischief.

Recommendations for Types of Humor

★ Use extremely silly humor—beyond "The Knights Who Say Ni" and into the territory of the Cheese Shop sketch. If you know the Cheese Shop sketch by heart, you are yourself uranian.
★ Try for Steven Wright's or Margaret Cho's type of humor.

Neptunian Prospects

Prospects with a prominent Neptune are likely to be:

★ intuitive
★ spiritual
★ reliant on others for a sense of self

Recommendations for Mischief Marketing Communications

★ Use imaginative, colorful language. Use poetry, if possible.
★ Emphasize the deeper meaning or significance of your offering.

Recommendations for Types of Humor

★ Tell jokes that have a larger meaning.
★ Steven Wright's humor appeals to people with a prominent Neptune.

Plutonian Prospects

Prospects with a prominent Pluto are likely to be:

★ intense
★ determined, even willful
★ mysterious, and fond of mystery
★ secretive
★ a bit power crazy
★ charismatic, if quietly so

Recommendations for Mischief Marketing Communications

★ Lend your offering an air of mystery.
★ Emphasize its power.
★ Emphasize the depth of its implications.

Recommendations for Types of Humor

★ Use dark, penetrating humor.
★ Use biting political satire.
★ Use humor that reflects a deep knowledge of human nature.
★ Avoid silly humor.

> *Two babies were born on the same day at the same hospital. They lay there and looked at each other. Their families came and took them away. Eighty years later, by a bizarre coincidence, they lay in the same hospital, on their deathbeds, next to each other. One of them looked at the other and said, "So. What did you think?"*
>
> —STEVEN WRIGHT

Mischievous Pop Quiz

1. An easy way to profile your prospect is to:
   a) spend years studying research techniques.
   b) sneak into CIA headquarters and use their computers while everyone is at lunch.
   c) ask a librarian to help you.

2. Birth-order theory:
   a) can be remarkably descriptive of some people.
   b) can give you insights into your VLP's personality, which you can later fold into your communications with her or him.
   c) is supported by a fair amount of research.
   d) all of the above.

3. Astrological art or theory:
   a) applies to some of the people some of the time.
   b) applies to some of the people all of the time.
   c) applies to all of the people some of the time.
   d) applies only to Abe Lincoln.

TOOLS OF THE MISCHIEF MARKETER

Now that know you something about your VLP, how do you get in touch with him or her? How can you find the information that will help you precisely mold your campaign to your target? Luckily, there are all kinds of tools you can use to carry out a good mischief marketing campaign.

Internet Tools

The Internet is tailor-made for mischief marketing. In fact, the Web might as well have been fashioned *by* mischief marketers *for* mischief marketers. Here are some reasons why.

You Can Assume Different Identities on the Internet

You can test your ideas experimentally without jeopardizing your reputation or being stopped by the prejudice that attaches to being unknown.

Of course, people like producer Robert Stigwood (see page 62) have been using pseudonyms (proxy identities) this way for centuries. But thanks to new encryption and anonymizing technology, it is now possible to create a proxy identity (a whole new you!) that satisfies the following conditions:

☛ Nobody can hijack your proxy and forge something under that name because you can give your work a unique digital signature. That signature may or may not be directly traceable to the real you (until *you* decide to reveal yourself).

Mining Mystery

*I*n 1967, a band released a new single and circulated it to radio stations but didn't put its name on the label. Producers told disc jockeys only that the name of the group started with a *B* and ended with an *S*. Assuming the new "mystery" single had really been recorded by the Beatles, the DJs played it, the public bought it, and "New York Mining Disaster, 1941" instantly became a huge hit. By the time the follow-up songs "Holiday" and "To Love Somebody" were released, everyone knew who the Bee Gees were.

In the mid-seventies, when the popularity of the Bee Gees had waned, producer Robert Stigwood deployed the same tactic, this time to change perceptions that biased listeners against the group. He released "Jive Talkin'"—again without putting a name on the label, again generating an aura of mystery, and again launching a surprise new hit. And so it happened that prejudice, pretension, and narrow-mindedness were usurped, at least for a moment (but all it takes is a moment), by mischief marketing.

☞ Nobody can take credit for your work except you, thanks to the power of digital authentication.

☞ You don't ever have to reveal who you really are unless you want to. If your campaign bombs, you can just abandon it.

☞ If your campaign succeeds, and you decide to take credit for your offering, you can prove that you—and only you—created the digitally authenticated work.

☞ You can use multiple proxies—think of an onion—that progressively protect (or reveal) your true identity in carefully orchestrated stages, which means you can test consumers' reactions at each stage of your mischief marketing experiment. You can calibrate your campaign and make midcourse corrections.

What I've just described is something called DRUID.

DRUID is an extremely powerful tactic that will soon be the tactic of choice for mischief marketers who want to have some serious fun.

Mischief Marketing with DRUID (deferred revelation of user's ID):

To test a new but potentially explosive mischief marketing campaign, use encryption and anonymizing technology to withhold your true identity until the moment comes (if it ever does) when you decide to reveal yourself.

My friend Uta, for example, holds a controversial point of view on a particular topic. In fact, it's so controversial that I can't even talk about it in this book. How can she market her point of view without jeopardizing her personal safety (or reputation) and that of her family? By using DRUID.

☞ First, Uta sets up her controversial website with an anonymizing host—a company that isn't interested in her true identity but will host her websites. She signs up for the service using a money order (that doesn't have her name on it, of course). And she uploads her Web pages to the server using publicly accessible computers (at libraries and cafes) so snoops can't trace her file transfer protocol ("FTP") activities through her Internet service provider.

☞ Second, Uta offers an encrypted file on her site. This file is what she will use later—if she chooses to identify herself as the author of the material on the site. (Only she has the key to this file.) Better yet, she publishes her public key on the site, too, so people can get in touch with her via anonymous E-mail and can be sure that the answers they receive are really from her, even though they don't know Uta Ellisatt.

☞ Third, she archives and encrypts a copy of her entire website and sends the file to a time-stamping service that can (later) validate that Uta—and only Uta—"certified" those documents at that date and time. This is an extra precaution to ensure that nobody else (say, at the host company) will be able to claim credit for Uta's site.

Idea Joggers

• Can you present your offering anonymously, in a way that makes people suspect you might be someone they already know and admire?
• Recognize when people think they've "got your number." Don't waste time trying to rehabilitate your image; that's a losing battle. Instead, create a new and better impression—then, when the time comes, reveal the truth.

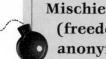

> ## Mischief Marketing by FIAT (freedom of information via anonymous transmission):
>
> To circulate banned or controversial information, use anonymous E-mail technology.

☛ Finally, she calls attention to her site (again using public computers), advertises it, sits back, and sees what happens. If she likes what she sees, Uta can claim credit for the mischief marketing campaign; if not, she can forget the whole thing.

Again, this is a simplistic presentation of the DRUID tactic, which is actually very powerful and flexible. For details, see mischiefmarketing.com.

Closely related to DRUID is FIAT. Both techniques can be used together. The easiest way to explain how FIAT works is, as usual, by telling a true story that shows how you might use it.

Not long ago, a Utah couple named the Tanners (their real name) posted some stuff on a website about a huge religious body we will call The Church of Holy Jesus Christ Almighty (not its real name; we don't dare infringe on any trademarks, and you'll soon see why). On the site, the Tanners told visitors where (at what URLs) to view some material that happened to be protected by the church's copyrights. Merely for providing the *location* of that information (not the copyrighted information itself), church lawyers promptly bullied the Tanners into court and sued them, successfully, for "contributory copyright infringement." It's as though you'd told a friend, "There are prostitutes at Washington Square Park," then later got arrested as a "contributory prostitute" for having indicated that location.

Big corporations and other control freaks are doing more and more of this kind of thing. It's called *cybersmearing*: using trademark and copyright law to intimidate critics like the Tanners—or you and me. Eventually, these giant organizations will erode the First Amendment to the Constitution, and gut our freedom of speech. Individuals (especially politicians) will soon start trademarking their names, too, which means you won't be able to say, "Senator Slubgob's voting record stinks" without infringing on the senator's trademark, for example.

But this won't happen right away. We still have a few years to use mischief marketing techniques like DRUID and FIAT.

If the Tanners want to transmit their message by FIAT, they can set up an account with an anonymous E-mailer or with a Web-surfing anonymizing service like ZeroKnowledge or Anonymizer. At the time of writing, Anonymizer and ZeroKnowledge were among the top services dedicated to shielding your real identity as you surf the Internet. But by the time you read this, they may already have competitors—or then again, someone may have started some "accidental" fires in the offices of all such firms. (You never know. Free speech threatens people.) Then the Tanners can tell website visitors, "If you're interested in *studying the legal issues* behind why we don't have the freedom of speech to tell you certain things about the church, sign up for our FIAT mailing list or post a message on alt.some.public.newsgroup that includes the code phrase 'I love the First Amendment; how about you?'" The italicized text indicates a legal fine point we can't discuss here. For details, see the mischiefmarketing.com website.

Then they can send anonymous information about the church to their subscribers along with legally "safe" information under their public name. The anonymous information should be sent at some random interval, not immediately after being requested. Should the question arise, the Tanners will want to claim that they sent only the harmless information. When the powerful church, or tobacco company, or whatever again tries to silence their critics (which they will), the bullying lawyers will first need to establish that the Tanners are in fact the people who sent the anonymous information. This is possible, of course, but very difficult technically. (And there are ways in which the Tanners can make it impossible.)

The result: the Tanners will have reclaimed their freedom of speech, and we will have access to information people tried to cover up. Again, this is a highly simplified presentation. It assumes, furthermore, that your motives are pure, that your information is accurate, and that the public really has a need to know (and wouldn't be harmed by) the information you're offering. In some cases, these assumptions may be wrong. As we've said before, you can use mischief marketing for good or evil.

On the Web, You Can Make Yourself Look as Big as a Major Corporation

At the moment, the Web is the most egalitarian communication space in the world. That means you as a mischief marketer still have a chance to use the Internet as a megaphone for your message or offering.

The Internet Lets You Hitch a Ride on Popular Subjects

Conventional marketing uses a concept called *comarketing*. It refers to how two companies sometimes get together on a marketing campaign because each wants to borrow a bit of the other's credibility or image to further its own brand. For example, if Nike sponsors an Olympic event, it acquires a redolence of athleticism, grace, and vigor. At the same time, the Olympic competition benefits because it acquires something of Nike's aura. In such a case, you could say that Nike and the Olympics are comarketing.

Similarly, the Internet lets you comarket with just about everyone because it's still legal for anyone to link to anyone else. It won't be legal forever, though. Historically, this kind of window of opportunity always closes as soon as the control freaks finally realize—as they are now—that you caught them with their pants down. At that point, they will concoct some "danger" that your freedom of expression supposedly harbors —communism, terrorism, pornography, child abuse, heresy, witchcraft, Judaism, Catholicism, atheism, evangelism, or whatever—and they will start censoring everything that falls within the penumbra of that cooked-up concept (which often has some shred of validity).

But the window of opportunity for universal, egalitarian comarketing is still open to you now, so by all means make use of it to associate your offering with anyone or anything you like.

You Can Parasite on the Internet

In mischief marketing we don't use the term comarketing because a mischief marketer may or may not expressly solicit the permission of the other, associated party. We call it *parasiting*. Parasiting means designing a website around a popular topic and then using that site as a gateway to your other sites.

Suppose you sell spittoons. Sure, you could set up a website called spittoon.com and hope that visitors show up, but that's not likely to happen spontaneously because the market for spittoons is limited.

Oh, it will soon become enormous, of course, because everything strange eventually becomes enormous. Look at Brando. But it isn't too big a market right now.

So what can you do to help sell your spittoons?

Well, you can start mischievously parasiting related products and services. For example, you can set up a website directed at defiant smokers, and on your site you could rally them to chew and spit tobacco in public as a kind of protest against the people who are upset about secondhand smoke. Then you could entice the smokers into viewing your catalog of beautiful, portable spittoons.

In other words, *you can hitch your offering to the bandwagon of the smoking debate*, which would be a kind of mischievous comarketing (or piggybacking or fly-tying). And if your site causes controversy, so much the better.

Meanwhile, you could set up another, harmless website that's all about brass. It could be an educational website with lots of good, solid information about brass. Then you could fly-tie (link) from that educational parasite to your catalog of brass spittoons. By associating your offering with brass products, you can hitch your offering to the bandwagon of brass lovers and collectors.

The example I just gave is ridiculous, of course. But, all kidding aside, whenever you mount an educational page that links to your offering, you're bound to get more traffic. The Internet makes it easy for you to do this.

Let me caution you about one thing, though: don't try to con people with this technique. Make sure your educational parasite is meaty and helpful. Don't try parasiting, say, a sudden, huge surge of pop interest in astrophysics by mounting a cheap page featuring little more than a picture of Stephen Hawking and a half-dozen "Fun Facts About the Solar System." If you try to fake it, your visitors will never come back.

You Can Bully-Bait Corporations or Politicians and Make the Resulting Fracas Newsworthy

The Internet can also be useful for baiting big-money bullies into coming after you (while you get press coverage of their bullying tactics). This is related to the tactic of parasiting a controversial issue.

The strategy is appearing more and more often in politics, where people are mounting parody websites that look just like the official websites of pompous politicians. The politicians stupidly take the bait and angrily try to shut down the critical websites—which of course only makes the candidates look like idiots and generates lots of free press for the mischief marketer who mounted the parody site.

Many good books about Internet marketing are available (see mischiefmarketing.com for a listing). Read a few of them and devise mischievous twists on the techniques they discuss.

You Can Circulate Clever Cartoons on the Internet

People love cartoons, and they love to pass them on to their friends. If you can create some mischievous cartoons and link them to your website, do so. The same goes for clever animations and videos.

This process is sometimes called *viral marketing* because the message in such cases tends to spread like a virus. Remember the dancing baby animation? That's a perfect example of viral marketing. In fact, the people who made that animation also used a form of DRUID. It was only when the animation had been circulated all over the world that the baby's creators (people at Kinetix, a division of AutoDesk) decided to raise their profile and capitalize on the craze.

You Can Start a Rumor in a Newsgroup

If you can start a rumor, maybe you can also mount a corrective, educational page that dispels that rumor (and links to your offering). At this point in history, it isn't hard to start rumors on the Internet. In fact, it's a snap. But please be sure you correct whatever rumor you start.

You Can Spark a Conspiracy Theory

Like their cousins, rumors, conspiracy theories also make good parasites.

My friend Uta has a conspiracy theory she almost believes. She suspects that the major pharmaceutical companies have discovered something useful about nicotine or some other component of tobacco.

But because nicotine is so readily available in tobacco, they don't want to announce their discovery until they can get tobacco outlawed or outpriced. Once they succeed in doing that, you'll have to go to a doctor to get a prescription for nicotine (or some derivative thereof) to cure whatever it cures, and the whole process will cost you a fortune. You won't be able to stuff your own capsules with tobacco because you won't be able to get tobacco anymore, or afford it.

Uta finds it curious that people are spending millions upon millions of dollars on ad campaigns designed to protect her health. (Uta is a smoker and should of course be imprisoned immediately.) "How nice of them!" Uta said to me, "I suppose that, any minute now, they'll also start spending millions upon millions of dollars to save us from another major cause of death—speeding—or from eating high-fat foods that cause killer heart disease. I'm sure those millions upon millions of loving, caring dollars are rolling in as we speak."

Experience tells Uta that whenever you see massive amounts of money being spent generously on you, it's not because your benefactors are so caring and wonderful. It's because they have some motive for "helping" you. Uta suspects, therefore, that the big pharmaceutical companies, having learned their lesson about aspirin (which they can't patent or overprice), are now applying what they learned to nicotine or to some other component in tobacco.

"Did you know that the *Wall Street Journal* reported not long ago that pharmaceutical companies have quietly been buying up tobacco farms?" Uta asked me (once she had reconnected her electronic voice box which, in her excitement, had tumbled to the floor). "Think about it, Ray. Even the reporter thought that was strange."

Anyhow, there you have an example of how to construct a conspiracy theory. If you can devise a plausible theory, people will link to your website, and from there you can shepherd them to whatever you're offering. Perhaps you're offering the truth.

You Can Parody a Movie or Advertisement

Again, your goal in such a case would be to get your parody circulated—and get people to link back to your website. If your parody is well done, you can combine this tactic with bully-baiting and try to get the people you're parodying to come after you for trademark violation. Just make sure you're protected legally.

For information on how to invoke that legal protection, familiarize yourself with the laws regarding trademarks, fair use, parody, and satire. Visit mischiefmarketing.com for links to legal resources.

> **Mischief Marketing Tip:**
>
> Know the law. Every mischief marketer needs to know something about the law. Some mischief marketers need to know a lot about the law.

Here are some of the legal questions you'll need to tackle:

★ What's the difference between violating someone's trademark and simply using the name of his or her product or service?
★ What First Amendment rights do you have to parody someone or something? What legal criteria are used to establish that something is a parody and therefore protected speech?
★ Is speech that calls for violence protected?
★ What constitutes libel or defamation?
★ Is it okay to deep link to a page on someone else's site?
★ What laws govern obscenity and pornography?
★ When you press an I Accept button on a website, are you really bound by the underlying agreement?
★ Can you specify, in a legally binding fashion, that certain people—or people in certain locales—may not view your site?

Because Internet law is still evolving, a good mischief marketer will try to keep up with recent rulings and may even decide to do something (mischievously) that will test a particular issue in court.

Non-Internet Tools

The Internet is a good mischief marketing tool, but many old-fashioned tools are available to you as well. In fact, the old-fashioned tools often work better than the newfangled electronic ones.

Take E-mail, for example. Isn't it incredibly irritating? Sure, it's useful, but tell the truth: isn't it nice to get something *physical* in the mail once in while, something written on real paper with a real pen by a real human? Well, guess what. Your prospects feel the same way.

So when you're taking inventory of your tools, consider these suggestions:

You Can Mount a Letter-Writing Campaign Directed at Your VLP

I'm talking about a ground mail campaign using beautiful paper, gorgeous envelopes, exquisite wrapping or filling (if you're mailing packages), and so on. Contemplate Michael Shurtleff's story in Chapter 8 to get a feel for this technique.

You Probably Know Someone Who Knows Someone Who Can Put You in Touch with Your VLP

The theory of "six degrees of separation" is a statistics-based idea which asserts that any two people in the world are separated socially (whether they know it or not) by not more than four or five people. (See Chapter 10.) That is, you probably know someone who knows someone (and so on) who knows Martha Stewart. Wouldn't that be wonderful? But you also know someone (etc.) who knows your VLP, so start asking around. You may be surprised to find out how well connected we all are on this planet.

You Can Produce an Interesting Press Release

My friend Sue Doanim once wrote a conventional press release but forgot to include the most basic information: namely, when and where the announced event was to take place. Once she spotted her embarrassing mistake, Sue realized that the only way to save face would be to use a mischief marketing weapon: the simple truth tactic (Chapter 12).

So she issued a second press release that essentially said, "The previous release failed to tell you when and where this event will take place. This is chiefly because, as a publicist, I am what is known in the trade as an incompetent jerk. If I were in a supermarket checkout line, you would recognize me immediately as the idiot clutching a fistful of coupons and fumbling with a checkbook in the Cash Only No Coupons line."

And what happened? Sue got something publicists often covet but too rarely get—prime-time television news coverage for her event.

You Can Perform an Odd Public Demonstration

This is an old trick, but it sometimes works.

In 1977, musician Elvis Costello was first starting out. He had signed a contract with Stiff Records, and he was happy about that, but he also wanted an international record deal. So he strapped a pignose amp on his back, planted himself outside the London hotel where CBS Records happened to be holding its annual international convention, and started playing. (He also got arrested.)

This was not a PR stunt but an authentic mischief marketing move because Costello first identified a very specific group of VLPs and conducted background research to find out where they were staying.

Conventional Marketing and Guerrilla Marketing Tools

Every mischief marketer should learn as much as possible about conventional and guerrilla marketing. There are lots of good concepts in these fields, ideas that have passed the test of time. Here are some examples:

★ Principle of integrating interests—a sales technique in which the salesperson knows the buyer's personal interests or buying motives and emphasizes these in the presentation rather than the features or benefits of the product. Also known as one-to-one marketing.

★ Kinesic communication—communicating through body movements such as head nodding, stance, posture, hand gestures, and so on. Nonverbal communication. Body language.

★ Advocacy advertising—a communication or message that presents information or a point of view on a controversial public issue, idea, or cause.

★ Microsegmentation—the process of dividing a market into smaller groups of customers on the basis of very narrowly defined needs and wants. In a sense, mischief marketing is actually microsegmentation and microtargeting taken to its logical limit, coupled with marketing by word of mouth.

★ Missionary selling—a sales technique in which the salesperson's role is to give information to an individual having the power to influence others to buy an offering, rather than to sell directly to that individual. A missionary salesperson is sometimes known as a detailer. Also called bottom line selling: selling to the top decision makers who value bottom-line improvements above all else.

★ Image differentiation—also known as branding. To create a competitive advantage, a company might differentiate itself from competitors by crafting a unique image. The specific image or personality it acquires derives from the unique mix of its logo, atmosphere, advertising, events, and personalities. Other types of differentiation include product differentiation, services differentiation, and personnel differentiation. In mischief marketing, the very strangeness of your approach constitutes a kind of differentiation.

For more information on how to incorporate conventional and guerrilla marketing tools into your mischievous campaigns, visit mischiefmarketing.com.

Mischievous *Pop* Quiz

1. When, you conduct a controversial mischief marketing campaign on the Internet under cover of anonymity, then later reveal (and prove) who you really are:
   a) you are using a mischief marketing technique called DRUID.
   b) you are bound to infuriate large corporations and government agencies so much that they'll lobby Congress to require every Internet user to be licensed, fingerprinted, and traceable through every link they visit on the Internet, until Big Brother succeeds in eradicating your privacy, and the privacy of all citizens, while preserving its own.
   c) you will be free at last—without jeopardizing your job, yourself, or your family—to speak truth to power.
   d) all of the above.

2. Parasiting is the mischief marketing practice of:
   a) building an informative and entertaining website around a hot topic in order to help attract users to your own website.
   b) gawking at things in the capital of France.
   c) using paranormal powers to indicate the source of a fact or statement; also known as paraciting.

3. Bully-baiting is the mischief marketing practice of:
   a) enticing some bully—usually a large, litigious corporation or a humorless politician—into attempting to suppress your freedom of speech, so you can attract the attention of the media when they sic their lawyers on you.
   b) turning the other cheek—toward the TV camera with the red light on.
   c) demonstrating that the First Amendment to the Constitution is alive and kicking, no matter how hard the control freaks try to crush it.
   d) all of the above.

CAPITAL AND NONCAPITAL RESOURCES

O kay, so now you know your VLP, and you've figured out how to reach her or him. But when should you spring into action? How much will it cost? How will you collect the resources you need to launch your campaign?

Raising Capital

Most mischief marketers aren't rich, so you'll want to start thinking about how to raise capital for your business. The Mother Teresa stories on pages 76 and 77 should get you thinking about creative ways of being frugal.

What can we learn from this tale? Isn't it about charity and fundraising? How can it possibly apply to marketing?

Well, in the first place, we can observe once again that mischief marketing is *not* just about marketing products or services. It is equally about marketing ideas. In this case, we see Mother Teresa "marketing" a very particular idea: how to help people who are less fortunate than we are.

> *Sir Sigmund [Sternberg], the only Jewish Papal knight, believes fervently in the power of religion as a force for good . . . . For him, Mother Teresa has an extremely good product "and there is no point in having a good product if you don't advertise it and market it."*
>
> —ANNE SEBBA
> *Mother Teresa: Beyond the Image*
> Doubleday, 1997.

The Old Woman on the Plane

On a plane bound for a poverty-stricken city in Mexico, the flight attendant prepares to serve lunch to an old woman and her traveling companion.

The old woman—a notoriously tough negotiator and seasoned international traveler—suddenly asks two questions: How much is the food worth in cash? And if she were to give up her lunch, would the airline donate the cash equivalent to charity?

Taken aback, the flight attendant consults the cockpit crew, who radio the ground crew, who contact the foodservice people, who call the purchasing agents, who phone the corporate executives. On and on it goes for about twenty minutes, the leathery old woman's queries bouncing from one head-scratching employee to another, around the world, and up and down thirty-five thousand feet of sky.

The answers finally come back: The food is worth about one dollar US. And yes, the airline would be happy to make the cash substitution. So the old woman gives up her lunch and accepts the donation. Within minutes, everyone else on board follows suit.

In the second place, we can observe that here is an example of how you can make use of limited resources.

> ### Mischievous Sourcing Tactic:
>
> Loaves and Fishes—Take a small opportunity and turn it into a big one.

The loaves and fishes tactic is a variation on the make lemonade tactic discussed in Chapters 11 and 12, except that where make lemonade entails merely making it look as though you have a lot of resources in order to boost your credibility, loaves and fishes goes a step further and entails transforming limited resources into abundant ones.

With loaves and fishes, you take a small opportunity and leverage it. In this case, Mother Teresa took some airline food and turned it into a dollar. That prompted other people to do the same. So the food became a dollar, and the dollar became a few hundred dollars, all in a matter of minutes. Over time, the telling and retelling of the story probably earned several thousand dollars for Mother Teresa in particular or for charitable causes in general. So we can probably say that, over the course of perhaps an

> ### Mischievous Sourcing Tactic:
>
> The Pasteur Tactic—Be prepared at every moment to take advantage of a chance marketing opportunity.

hour, Mother Teresa turned a small lunch into thousands of dollars.

Mischief marketing involves being constantly prepared, constantly ready to act on the spur of the moment. That way, you can instantly take advantage of lucky breaks and chance opportunities.

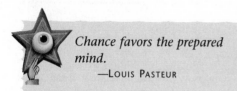

Chance favors the prepared mind.
—LOUIS PASTEUR

Mother Teresa was prepared to work for her cause twenty-four hours a day, seven days a week. She didn't stop being prepared just because she happened to be on a plane. Does this mean you have to work all the time at marketing your offering? Of course not! If you do nothing but work, you'll burn out. Your family and friends will suffer, and your work will, too.

No, this tale certainly does not suggest you should work all the time. But it does suggest you may want to be *prepared* to work at all times. And by work we mean marketing, selling, or presenting your ideas, products, services—and yes, like Mother Teresa, your deepest religious, spiritual, or social values. Your offering.

You can often use humor to raise capital. And as a mischief marketer, you should be looking for opportunities to use humor whenever possible in any situation.

Raising Money through Internet Direct Public Offerings

There's a new way of raising money that will soon become real hot, especially among mischief marketers. It has to do with Internet-based direct public offerings (DPOS).

When the plane lands, the woman asks the crew what they plan to do with the untouched food. They plan to throw it out. So she elbows her traveling companion and says, "Go back in there and get that food." He does, and she promptly hands out a hundred airline lunches to the hungry people greeting her at the airport.

That hard-driving old woman's name? Mother Teresa of Calcutta.

Mother Teresa Holds up Grocery Clerk

*H*er quest to serve the poorest of the poor sometimes brought Mother Teresa close to breaking the law while conducting her mischievous marketing.

Once, having bought $800-worth of goods for the poor in a supermarket, she refused to move from the checkout until someone else in the queue paid for them. A fund-raiser of Mother Teresa's virtuosity could not merely decline into the peaceful embrace of God she recommended for her patients; she had a duty to survive.

—"Mother Teresa (Obituary)"
The Economist,
September 13, 1997

Using Humor to Raise Money

W hen you have nothing to lose, mischief marketing may be the best thing you can do. Limited only by guts and imagination, it's available to anyone and everyone.

He stands on a corner near Union Square, one of many homeless men—and a few women—appealing for money on a summer weekend. But instead of printing a generic "Homeless and hungry" request on cardboard, he lightens his plea with humor, calling out, "Spare some change for the residentially challenged?"

A block away, another needy man rattles coins in his paper cup and holds a sign bearing a joking message: "My wife's been kidnapped. I'm short 98 cents for ransom." Nearby, a third man also tries for laughs by waving a colorful whale hand puppet— and a cup—at pedestrians.

Humor is not typically the stock-in-trade of the dispossessed. But like merchants seeking to attract customers with advertising jingles, these desperate citizens of the street hope their ploys will capture the attention—and money—of shoppers, tourists, and convention-goers.

> —MARILYN GARDNER
> "When the Homeless Use Humor
> to Fill Their Empty Cups"
> *Christian Science Monitor,* July 8, 1998

Humor usually helps improve difficult situations (economic and otherwise). Why? Because people run away from problems. They're afraid to look at them. Secretly, most people believe that if they look at other people's difficulties, they might "catch" them—the way they might catch the flu. Humor defangs this fear.

Idea Joggers

- How can you present your need for funding in a humorous way?
- How can you poke fun at your capital-raising effort in a way that doesn't really derogate your project?
- Hint: use an accomplice to discover what people are already thinking about you or your offering. Then use that information as the basis for an application of the simple truth tactic—with a dose of humor added for good measure.

Financial Liposuction

S olarAttic, Inc. is not a sexy Internet Siren, but a small, solid, rather conventional company.

For years, SolarAttic struggled to hit the bull's-eye with its proven products. But alas, its wares were not high-tech. And even though sales at the company were far more promising than at most Silly/Con Valley start-ups, the money people whom founder Ed Palmer approached for help—angels, venture capitalists, investment bankers, brokers—were too busy running around spurting seed capital into various profit-barren, painted ladies of the Valley; too busy, that is, to

Mischievous Fund-Raising Tip:

Keep track of the process of doing direct public offerings. And if you're a small investor yourself, find out everything you can about this new mechanism.

In a direct public offering, you offer shares of stock in your company directly to the public. That is, you bypass the middlemen, the bureaucratic old boys (BOBS) who have traditionally controlled the stock markets, serviced each other onanistically, and created endless

The realization of ultra-low-cost, wide-open stock offerings—a pure, frictionless transfer of money from the public to a company—may ultimately become one of the most powerful applications of the Internet. It's turbocapitalism: for ordinary investors, a chance to get in on the ground floor of even tiny, distant, or obscure companies; for underfunded, non-Web start-ups, an opportunity to get their story out to people who might be willing to take a modest gamble.

—DAVID H. FREEDMAN
"Got Money? Businesses
Search for Investors in
Cyberspace"
Inc., September 16, 1999

even glance at a firm like his.

So Palmer decided to thumb his nose at the financiers. He decided to do something so cutting edge, so "out there" both in terms of technology and commerce, that even the most strung-out tech junkies are scared to try it (at the moment). In fact, only one company, Spring Street Brewing, had really tried it before.

He decided to go public by using the Internet—and, eventually, *only* the Internet—to find SolarAttic investors. And we're talking about small investors, too; regular folks who'd like to get into a growth area that the big boys haven't yet locked up tight; workaday investors who can put up maybe a thousand here, five hundred there; real people.

In other words, Palmer mischief marketed his offering directly to the people, daring to go where even high-tech angels feared to tread.

Turnering on a Dime

*I*t is May 21, 1979, and Ted Turner is wired.

It is just moments before his press conference announcing the startup of CNN, and he's about to market a company that doesn't exist. That alone would be mischievous enough, but there's more.

Turner wants to sign the highly credible journalist, Daniel Schorr, and he needs to do it immediately. Schorr is essential to the success of his start-up. Turner must sign someone credible before this press conference or his whole project will seem ridiculous.

Here's how he does it.

Schorr had resigned from CBS in 1976, when the network failed to support him in a historic confrontation over freedom of the press. He had refused to reveal his sources at the CIA in the Pentagon papers case. Cited for perjury, Schorr stood his ground and won.

"I absolutely will not do anything I don't want to do," he told Turner. "Nothing I feel might compromise my professional standards." He looked Turner straight in the eye, fully expecting him to blink. "Write that down and I'll sign it," Turner exclaimed, shoving a piece of hotel stationery into Schorr's hand.

barriers to entry for the little guy—always, of course, in the name of "protecting" us from fraud (although, to be fair, the BOBS do in fact protect people from fraud now and then).

Not all the kinks have been worked out of the DPO process yet. So don't go hog wild about it until you're sure you know what you're doing. It's a radically new way to raise capital. Do your homework first. But take the plunge if you can.

For more information on Internet direct public offerings, visit mischiefmarketing.com.

Timing the Launch of Your Campaign

In mischief marketing, timing the launch of your campaign and raising capital resources are not usually separate activities, as they might be in a conventional campaign. That's because in a mischief marketing campaign you're usually racing against the budgetary clock, sometimes with creditors nipping at your heels. When is the right time to launch a campaign? If you've planned it meticulously and all systems are go, how quickly should you act?

Mischievous Timing Tactic:

Remember the Eleventh Hour Principle—When you go out on a limb with a mischief marketing project, your results are likely to bear fruit only at the very last minute—the eleventh hour.

This is a general principle in life—not just in mischief marketing—a principle that most people never grasp and that almost nobody discusses in the many otherwise fine self-help books that are on the shelves today.

Nature likes to do things at the last minute. That's why in so many myths, stories, plays, movies, fairy tales, and novels salvation always comes at the last minute. Such stories are exciting, and they ring true because they reflect the truth we know in our hearts. They show us that many important projects tend to fall into place only at the last minute.

Ted Turner knew this. He set up a press conference for a company that hardly existed. Then, at the last possible minute, when it must have seemed to him that he wasn't going to have anything to announce to the press after all, he met Schorr and signed him up with no questions asked. That last-minute action permitted Turner to make something out of nothing, and he was able to take that action because he instinctively understood the eleventh hour principle: Nature likes to do things at the last minute.

If you don't grasp this as deeply as Ted Turner did, what happens? You get discouraged, of course. You don't "go the distance," as the whispering voice in *Field of Dreams* says. You give up. You get depressed. You lose energy. You fall into despair. You settle for a job you hate. You need to continually remind yourself that if what you're doing is authentically important, the chances are great that it will all come together for you only at the last possible minute.

Take the guy who wrote the screenplay for the hugely successful film *Dances with Wolves*. I heard that by the time he sold the screenplay, he was almost broke. Another writer on a different popular film was broke, too, when he sold his screenplay. The check arrived in the mail the same day he received an eviction notice from the landlord. How's that for last minute?

[Schorr speaking:] "I became CNN's first editorial employee, with an ironclad, five-year contract. Probably the tightest anybody had ever seen. Just so Ted could go ahead with that press conference. . . . When Turner signed that agreement with me, there was no CNN, no structure, no organization, no office, no anything. This guy had the reputation of a buccaneer, but later on I came to understand that he was really serious about doing something worthwhile."

—PORTER BIBB
It Ain't as Easy as It Looks: Ted Turner's Amazing Story
Crown Publishers, 1993

If you want to make God laugh, tell Him your plans.

If you cannot accept this principle, if you insist on safety, security, and a guarantee that everything will happen according to your preconceived schedule with no surprises, then you don't want to continue reading this book.

Faith as a Marketing Resource

Mischievous Timing Tactic:

Fake It 'til You Make It—If you don't have enough faith to carry you through a project to the very last, despairing minute, act as though you do.

People have a lot of serious misunderstandings about the nature of faith. They confuse having great faith with having a big ego. To some of her critics, Mother Teresa—a woman of enormous faith—seemed to be on an ego trip, a power trip. Several critics have said such things about her. Of course, you'd have to be a little dull-witted to think that someone who spent almost every day bathing filthy lepers and wiping up vomit and pus from dying people was on an ego trip. But nevertheless, this is what Mother Teresa's critics say about her. Why? Because it's their job to say things like that.

Are you reluctant to display true faith in your offering? Are you hesitant to walk around, as Maya Angelou says, ". . . like I've got oil wells / Pumping in my living room"? Is it because you're afraid people will say you're egotistical? In other words, are you so proud of looking humble that you must look humble at all costs?

Misunderstandings about the true nature of faith go hand in glove with corollary confusions about the true nature of humility. People often think being humble means putting themselves down or selling themselves short. But that's false humility. Don't stop yourself from having faith in your offering or in yourself just because it might look like egotism to someone else. Many good, wonderful people are stopped in life just because they don't want to look prideful. This is sad.

Do you think Jesus was always humble? Many people think so, but do you think he always *looked* humble? How about when he was knocking over the tables in the temple? Do you think he looked humble then? Or how about Dr. Martin Luther King, Jr. when he was marching against civil injustice? Do you think he looked humble at those moments?

Those who say "Who do you think you are?" paint heroes with a brush that makes them look prideful, egotistical, and power hungry. They can make anybody look full of pride and ego—except themselves, of course (they always represent themselves as towering models of humility and "journalistic" honesty).

If you think you need to have a big ego to have faith in your offering, forget it. You don't need a big ego to have faith. You don't need pride. You don't even need confidence. You need just two things: the ability to act as though you have a lot of faith and the ability to put up with critics who accuse you of being egotistical and uppity. That's all you need.

Leveraging Your Resources

I've said that mischief marketing is mostly for people of modest means, but maybe I spoke too soon. Actually, the question of budgeting really becomes important in mischief marketing when someone has a lot of money. It's strange, yet it's true, because if you have a lot of money, you may be tempted to do something too big or too expensive. For instance, you may decide to pay for a huge billboard featuring what you think is a mischievous message—you know, some grammatically tricky thing like: "*The Birds* Is Coming."

But unless you happen to be Alfred Hitchcock (who advertised *The Birds* in precisely this way), big gestures do not make a mischief marketing campaign. The Hitchcock campaign is the exception that proves the rule.

> ### Mischief Marketing Rule:
> Mischief marketing is about designing the exception that proves the rule.

Leveraging the Legends

*T*hese days, almost everyone recognizes how barbaric it is to wear fur. After all, to make an average-sized, full-length mink coat, for example, you have to sacrifice about fifty or sixty animals. The idea that it's somehow classy to walk around parading the forensic evidence of so much senseless killing would be hilarious if it were not just hideous. That's what many animal rights activists believe, anyhow.

But it was not always this way. Mink coats were once considered elegant. Years ago, when Blackglama executives wanted to market their fur coats, they didn't have a lot of money to spend on their campaign. They figured out a mischievous way to get famous people to endorse the dead creatures' pelts almost for free by designing one of the most successful and longest-running ad campaigns in history: *"What becomes a legend most?"* This brilliant campaign showed venerable and often genuinely talented celebrities such as Judy Garland modeling minks in pictures done (usually) by superstar photographer Richard Avedon. It was a kind of semiotic sausage factory that took has-beens and ground them up with concepts like old, classic, and famous until they oozed out legendary at the other end.

The ad campaign itself became so well known that it was discussed in magazines and books, effectively extending its reach to millions of extra people at no cost to the company. By then, a mischievous feedback loop was in effect: (a) famous people loaned their lessening fame to a campaign, which (b) made the campaign itself more famous, so that (c) the campaign in turn could loan its fame to even less famous people, which (d) made the less famous more famous, so that (e) the campaign itself became more famous, so that (f) even more famous people wanted to be part of the campaign. And so on.

As a result of this loop, and even though the models' payment for appearing in these ads usually amounted to nothing more than a coat, more and more stars and comeback seekers became so eager to be depicted as legends that they practically hunted down the minks themselves. In other words, it was by understanding the needs of these particular VLPs, and by mischief marketing to them accordingly (via a species of parasiting or comarketing) that Blackglama parlayed a relatively limited budget into millions of dollars' worth of surplus publicity.

Idea Joggers

- Can you find a promising VLP seeking a comeback, preferably one with genuine talent? You'd be surprised to learn how many so-called has-beens are really prodigies whose fame worked against them by hiding their sensibility in the shadow of their celebrity. Brian Wilson of the Beach Boys comes to mind, but there are many others. They're fame's fallen angels, potential phoenixes waiting to become rediscovered radicals.
- If you can find such a person, how can you help your VLP market him- or herself while comarketing your own offering in the process?
- Blackglama staked out linguistic territory by borrowing and nearly branding the

Those of us who don't have money to burn have to leverage our resources and use them wisely in our mischief marketing.

When once a chairman of a multinational company came to see me, to offer me a property in Bombay, he first asked: "Mother, how do you manage your budget?"

I asked him who had sent him here. He replied: "I felt an urge inside me."

I said: "Other people like you come to see me and say the same. It was clear God sent you, Mr. A, as He sends Mr. X, Mrs. Y, Miss Z, and they provide the material means we need for our work. The grace of God is what moved you. You are my budget."

—MOTHER TERESA

concept of "legend." Others, many of them journalists, have created, packaged, or simply given a name to categories like rising star, pundit, heart-throb, politico, hacker, mover and shaker, entre-preneur, infotainer. And the name game goes on even as we speak. For instance, a national maga-zine not long ago pro-posed a new classification and christened it "Titans of 'Tude." It comprises influ-ential people whose work is characterized by humor and a sometimes cranky or eccentric attitude.

- Can you borrow an old classification and make it look new? Can you invent a new one and name it?
- What VLPs might want to be baptized into your new class at little or no cost to you?
- How far can you go before critics say, "Stop! You can't extend a concept that far!"?

You could argue that, ultimately, all of mar-keting—in fact, all of economics—is about cre-ating the kind of positive feedback loop that Blackglama achieved. The question for the authentic mischief marketer is whether your hall of mirrors, if you decide to create one, is moral or malevolent.

In a malevolent feedback loop, big banks and corporations shore each other up and con-spire to exert more and more power over small businesses and disadvantaged workers. Even-tually, however, their house of cards collapses, usually when they begin to mistrust *each other* because they know full well that they're all crooks. The result is a stock market crash or a savings and loan fiasco.

In a moral amplification of budgetary resources, however, the end result is a win for everyone.

Take the story told about young Thomas Edison, in which his mom suddenly got sick and needed emergency surgery. There wasn't enough time to get her to the hospital, and the house was too dark for the surgeon to work, so Edison amplified the resources he had. He got all the oil lamps and all the mirrors from all over the house into the dining room. Then he arrayed the oil lamps around the table and put the mirrors behind them. The light shone into the mirrors and bounced from mirror to mirror until there was a field of brilliance above the table and the doctor could work on his patient. The surgery was successful and Mrs. Edison's life was saved. Everybody won. Eventually, they say, this event inspired Edison to invent the electric light. So you and I won, too.

This templative tale tells us that we should never confuse resources with money. Don't amplify money; amplify resources—both capital and noncapital. If money helps you amplify your resources, so much the better, but remember this: *All the money in the world could not have helped Edison on that fateful night when his mom lay dying.*

In fact, you don't need money to do mischief marketing. Use your intellectual capital, your social capital, your creative capital. Use real resources, not just some symbol of resources—which is all that money is, anyhow: a paper symbol of real resources. When you're hungry, you don't go around collecting and eating menus, do you? So don't go around collecting money. Collect resources instead, including money.

And if that doesn't work, save yourself some work and use Mother Teresa's method. Believe me, it's much more cost-effective.

Mischievous Pop Quiz

1. The loaves and fishes tactic entails:
   a) taking stories from the Gospels and using them to preach hatred and intolerance.
   b) taking the resources you have and amplifying or leveraging them.
   c) taking advantage of even small opportunities.
   d) both (b) and (c).

2. Louis Pasteur once said:
   a) "Chance favors the prepared mind."
   b) "Synchronicity prepares the favorable mind."
   c) "Chances are your chances are awfully favorable."

3. If you don't have faith in yourself:
   a) fake it 'til you make it.
   b) act as though you have faith in yourself.
   c) avoid superstitiously thinking that if you let yourself believe in miracles they might stop happening to you; it's okay to believe in miracles, no matter how you choose to define them.
   d) all of the above.

KNOWING
WHAT CAN
GO WRONG

I n every trade—from flower arranging to silicon chip design—the
professionals generally know a thing or two that we amateurs don't.
It's not just that they know shortcuts or tricks that the rest of us don't know,
although they do. What's really important is that experts know what can
(and probably will) go wrong.

No matter how wonderful your marketing plan, no matter how inspiring your mission, no matter how well-engineered your goals or your
unique selling proposition, you're going to fall on your face if you don't
know (as well as any professional would know) what can go wrong with
a mischief marketing campaign.

*An expert is a man who has made all the mistakes
which can be made in a very narrow field.*

—NIELS BOHR
Quoted in *The Harvest of a Quiet Eye*
Institute of Physics, 1977

In this part of the book we're going to concentrate on the things that
can go wrong when you embark on a mischief marketing campaign. And
in this field, of all the things that can go wrong, psychological and social
factors are the most important and, therefore, potentially the most
troublesome.

The Estée Lauder story (on page 90) is interesting, but the secrets that
contribute to a successful mischief marketing campaign have nothing to
do with how this person snuck onto a movie lot or that person spilled

Clumsy Estée

Cosmetics queen Estée Lauder was one of the greatest entrepreneurs ever. Starting at the bottom, she built an empire that today is worth over three billion dollars. Here's how she managed (mischievously of course) to land an important buyer for her first perfume, even though the buyer was a real Cerberus-type watchdog who tried to block her efforts:

By 1960, the ever-aggressive Lauder had launched an international program and personally broke the prestigious Harrod's account in London. She was forced to resort to some sales creativity to break the prestigious Galleries Lafayette account in Paris. When she could not get the manager to agree to stock her products, Lauder "accidentally" spilled her Youth Dew [her first fragrance] on the floor during a demonstration in the middle of a crowd. The appealing scent was pervasive and aroused customer interest and comments. The manager capitulated and gave her an initial order.

—GENE N. LANDRUM
Profiles of Female Genius: Thirteen Creative Women Who Changed the World Prometheus Books, 1994

perfume on the floor. Evocative or inspiring though such stories may be, they tell us little about how to do something authentically creative and original. No, the factors in mischief marketing that really matter are not technical or logistical. They're not "tricks." They are the creative, dynamic factors *behind* the tales.

> ## Mischief Marketing Tip:
>
> It's the soul that counts. The most important factors that determine the success of any mischief marketing campaign are psychological, psychosocial—even spiritual.

These things are more important than learning mischievous tricks because what drives a good mischief marketing campaign is almost identical to what drives your creativity. And your creativity is heavily influenced by psychological, psychosocial, and spiritual phenomena. In other words, to do mischief marketing, you need to be creative. But to be creative, you need to take care of yourself psychologically (and physically, too, of course).

There are many good books on developing your creativity, and you will find the best of them described at mischiefmarketing.com. There's no point in duplicating the material here. What I will do instead is discuss some factors that are rarely discussed in any of those books. These are the factors that affect or impinge upon your ability to be creative. They are things we have in common with many other people but that, for some reason, we tend to think are peculiar to us. In other words, they're *public* matters that we sadly mistake for *private* matters.

At one time, believe it or not, people thought cancer was something private, even something to be ashamed of. If you got cancer back in the 1950s or 1960s, you tried not to talk about it. It was considered a personal matter. It was the same with alcoholism, mental illness, and even pregnancy. I'm sure you can name at least three things in your life that you secretly believe are "personal" problems unique to you or your family even though you know they are really common to millions of people.

The point is this: we human beings take a lot of things personally that are not personal at all. Those are the things I'm going to discuss now—factors that affect your ability to be creative, factors that you may mistakenly believe are personal, generic factors that affect anyone who tries to do anything creative. And of these psychological factors, the most important one is the Gethsemane effect.

Confronting the Gethsemane Effect

In the story about Home Depot (page 92), notice how the founders of that hugely successful chain suffered through an early period in which they felt betrayed.

There are countless stories like this that tell how a company got started, how hard it was to get funding, how nobody believed in it, and so on. Sure, there's a mischievous trick embedded in that Home Depot story (page 92) about the empty boxes they piled up to make the store look well stocked, but what do all stories of this type really teach you? To pile up empty boxes? Of course not.

They teach you that when you are on the verge of doing something important but difficult, people around you will often fail to recognize or appreciate what you're doing. That's the Gethsemane effect.

Idea Joggers
- What can *you* do to demonstrate your offering "accidentally"?
- Can you enlist your friends to play the role of strangers interested in your offering so that your prospect will take a second look?

Home Depot Founders Betrayed, Snubbed, Get Rich, Get Even

*O*ver the past 20 years, Bernard Marcus and Arthur Blank have transformed a few ragtag stores in Atlanta into the nationwide profit-making empire known as Home Depot Inc. Now the emperors of home-improvement retailing have decided to tell their tale, pay tribute to colleagues—and settle a few scores.

In Built from Scratch, . . . the two self-described regular guys swing a 2-by-4 at Sanford Sigoloff, a corporate turnaround artist who dubbed himself Ming the Merciless after a character in a Flash Gordon movie and proved the point by firing Messrs. Marcus and Blank from a company he once ran. They berate bankers who refused loans to Home Depot in the early days. . . .

More gently, they tweak Ross Perot's ears for blowing a chance to invest $2 million in 1978 for a 70% interest in the company—a stake that would be valued at more than $60 billion at today's stock price. . . .

In the early days, cash was short. Store employees used empty boxes to create the illusion of fully stocked shelves. . . .

Mr. Perot doesn't dispute the book's account. "They love to tell that story," he says cheerfully. The entrepreneur and some-time presidential candidate admits that he missed a rare investment opportunity but doesn't sound bitter about it. "I've been more than blessed in terms of financial success," he says. "I'm not just seeing how many marbles I can pile up before I die."

Messrs. Marcus and Blank have piled up plenty of marbles. Mr. Marcus's 2.6% stake in the company is now valued at about $2.4 billion, and Mr. Blank's 1.4% interest at $1.3 billion. Both are giving large amounts away to charities. They even find a charitable word for their former nemesis, Mr. Sigoloff. "Without Sandy," Mr. Marcus writes, "where would we be today?"

—JAMES R. HAGERTY
Wall Street Journal, February 19, 1999

That is, you're probably going to experience loneliness. You're probably going to feel abandoned or betrayed by friends and family. And you're probably going to wish you never got yourself into the business, project, job, marriage, partnership, or marketing task in which you happen to be engaged. You won't have these feelings all the time, but you will feel them often enough to make you want to throw in the towel.

The Gethsemane effect takes its name from the story about a famous rabbi who successfully marketed—both mischievously and perhaps miraculously—a number of ideas that still resonate for millions of people even today, thousands of years after his campaign.

They went to a place called Gethsemane, and [the famous rabbi who marketed many important ideas] said to his disciples, "Sit here while I pray."

He took Peter, James, and John along with him, and he began to be deeply distressed and troubled. "My soul is overwhelmed with sorrow to the point of death," he said to them. "Stay here and keep watch."

Going a little farther, he fell to the ground and prayed that if possible the hour might pass from him.

"Father," he said, "everything is possible for you. Take this cup from me. Yet not what I will, but what you will."

Then he returned to his disciples and found them sleeping. "Simon," he said to Peter, "are you asleep? Could you not keep watch for one hour? Watch and pray so that you will not fall into temptation. The spirit is willing, but the body is weak." Once more he went away and prayed the same thing.

When he came back, he again found them sleeping, because their eyes were heavy. They did not know what to say to him.

Returning the third time, he said to them, "Are you still sleeping and resting? Enough!"

—MARK 14:32–41

Evil Mischief Marketing— CREEPing

*C*REEP = CRedibility Erosion through Extremist Positioning.

One of the most effective (but least morally acceptable) ways to market your offering is to discredit the offering of your competition. And one of the most powerful, deeply cunning, and *certainly* immoral ways to do so is to become a CREEPer for the competition's views. This is especially true in the marketplace of ideas.

A CREEPer is a sort of mole. You become a CREEPer whenever you adopt a position on an issue that is so ridiculous and extreme that it embarrasses everyone who holds a more reasonable position on that issue. In that way, you can successfully erode the credibility of the entire enterprise.

For example:

- If you wanted to CREEP the pro-life movement, you would shoot innocent people in an abortion clinic.
- If you were a CREEPer for the Bible, you would shout repeatedly that anyone who doesn't take it literally is doomed. That would deter people from reading the Bible better than almost anything else you could do.

Enough! That's what you, too, will feel like saying at certain key moments in your quest or project.

> *Whenever we find that our religious life is making us feel that we are good—above all, that we are better than someone else—I think we may be sure that we are being acted on, not by God, but by the devil.*
>
> —C. S. LEWIS
> *Mere Christianity*
> Macmillan, 1952

Parents are a common source of the Gethsemane effect. The famous chemist Kary Mullis tells a story that illustrates this. He invented the technique that makes it possible to multiply tiny quantities of DNA in order to make accurate identifications of samples. In the following passage, Mullis describes what happened the day the press announced he had won the Nobel Prize for chemistry.

Friends began arriving with champagne, and the party began. That afternoon I finally reached my mother. I wanted to tell her to stop sending me articles about DNA, since I had now won the Nobel Prize for my expertise on that subject. My mother often mailed me articles from *Reader's Digest* about advances in DNA chemistry. No matter how I tried to explain it to her, she never grasped the concept that I could have been writing those articles, that something I had invented made most of those DNA discoveries possible. She probably hoped that winning the Nobel Prize might enable me to be published some day in *Reader's Digest*.

—KARY MULLIS
Dancing Naked in the Mind Field
Pantheon Books, 1998

But the sources of the Gethsemane effect are not restricted to your mom or dad. It could show up through your husband, your wife, your kids, your best friend, your coworkers, or your boss—anybody you know.

In the case of Federal Express founder Fred Smith, it showed up through his sisters, who—goaded by their lawyers, no doubt—banded together soon after the 1973 launch of FedEx and sued Smith for "misinvesting" the family money. In the case of the founders of Home Depot, it was their boss who betrayed them and prospective investors such as Ross Perot who abandoned or ignored them.

Then there's what happened to Satoshi Tajiri, the creator of the hugely popular Pokémon phenomenon. By 1996, five of his employees had abandoned him because they didn't think Pokémon was going to make any money. (Imagine their embarrassment today.) Even Tajiri's parents didn't have much faith in his endeavors at first, although they later came around.

But whoever happens to become the vehicle for this phenomenon in your life, the end result is the same: you're going to feel betrayed and abandoned by somebody. That's how the Gethsemane effect works, and it occurs far more often than you might suppose.

- If you're CREEPing feminism, you would preach that all men are hateful scum, try to ban everything they're interested in, and declare that all little boys have attention deficit disorder. That would discredit feminism in general.
- If you're CREEPing the gay rights movement, you would "out" famous people against their will, or claim publicly that older men should sleep with boys. That would erode the value of gay rights in the marketplace of ideas.

It is more difficult to pull off this evil trick in the marketplace of products and services (business) because people in business are familiar with such tactics and will stop you. For instance, if you officially work for Coca-Cola but are really a mole for Pepsi, and if you insanely attempt to CREEP Coca-Cola by declaring it the "Official Drink of Abortion Clinic Killers," Coca-Cola will simply fire you. So CREEPers tend to confine their tactics to politics and religion, where they work magnificently.

Because CREEP activity violates many (if not all) of the mischief marketing commandments, it does not qualify as mischief marketing.

Satoshi Tajiri [was] a young outcast who, as a boy living just outside Tokyo, collected insects and other tiny creatures of field, pond and forest. In a nation of ultraconformists, he was a misfit who didn't even dream of college. His father tried to get him a job as an electrical-utility repairman. He refused. No one expected him to go very far, even when he came up with the game after six trying years. . . . "My parents cried that I had become a delinquent."

—*Newsweek*, November 22, 1999

*When Christ said: "I was hungry and you fed me,"
he didn't mean only the hunger for bread and for
food; he also meant the hunger to be loved. Jesus
himself experienced this loneliness. . . . The same hunger,
the same loneliness, the same having no one to be accepted
by and to be loved and wanted by. Every human being in
that case resembles Christ in his loneliness; and that is the
hardest part, that's real hunger.*

—MOTHER TERESA

Mischief Marketing Preparatory Tactic:

Accept the Gethsemane effect. Realize that it's normal. Don't take it personally.

The Gethsemane effect happens to everyone who tries to accomplish anything, whether it's giving birth to a child, starting a business, or passing a law to stop people from playing Chopsticks. Don't let it hang you up.

When a woman is delivering a child, she is likely to experience the effect firsthand. She's struggling to bring this new life into the world, and no one can help her do it. She is essentially on her own. Although doctors, drugs (and a husband's hand to hold) may be of some aid and comfort, she's the only one who can bring this project to life. Just as you are the only one who can bring your project to life.

So, when you take on a new business endeavor, you may find it helpful to think of yourself as a mother who's about to deliver a child. Expect to endure pain, alienation, frustration, and anger. But know also that, in the end, you'll feel a rousing sense of accomplishment, joy, and relief. It means the baby that you carried, dreamed about, planned for, and hoped for is about to be born. Dwelling on all the work you had to do by yourself will stop you at precisely those moments when you need to "keep on keeping on."

Confronting your destiny—sweating out life's crises and transitions (even happy ones)—will sometimes be an excruciatingly lonely and painful state of affairs that no one close to you can fully understand or help you with. That's what the Gethsemane effect is about.

Be good and you will be lonesome.

—MARK TWAIN
Following the Equator
Ecco Press, 1992

Confronting the Sabotage Syndrome

Another tactic you need to know is how to confront the sabotage syndrome, which is closely related to the Gethsemane effect.

There are four kinds of sabotage that are relevant in this context: that which comes from people close to you, from acquaintances, from your prospect's watchdogs, and from within yourself. Needless to say, the most insidious one is the last. But let's take them in order.

Sabotage from People Close to You

Whenever you try to do something that goes beyond the goals and dreams to which most people limit themselves, people closest to you may unconsciously sabotage your efforts in subtle ways. It is the Gethsemane effect taken one step further.

When I say sabotage, I don't mean something paranoid and crazy. I don't mean, for example, that your friends will transmogrify into Mafia

Mischief Marketing in Science: Sophie's Choice Ruse

*I*n the 1700s, if you were a woman interested in math, many people thought you were mentally ill. That's why, when Sophie Germain (born in 1776) started staying up all night to study number theory and calculus, her father confiscated her candles, hid her clothes, and made sure she didn't get any heat. The poor guy thought his daughter was going nuts.

None of this stopped Germain, who kept a secret cache of candles and wrapped herself in bedclothes in order to continue her work. But when the time came for her to go beyond books and study at a real university, she was stuck. The prestigious school that would have been perfect for her accepted only men.

So Germain mischief marketed her way into the Ecole Polytechnique by assuming the identity of a former student, Antoine-August Le Blanc. The school didn't know that Le Blanc had left Paris and that the person now getting his lecture notes (and solving his problems) was really Sophie.

All went well until the course supervisor, famed mathematician Joseph Lagrange, noticed one day that Le Blanc, not the brightest bulb on the tree, had suddenly turned into an extraordinary mathematician. Lagrange soon learned Germain's true identity and took her under his wing. She no longer had to pretend to be Le Blanc with him. But she did use this mischief marketing device at least one other time—when communicating with Carl Friedrich Gauss.

Germain's work on Fermat's Last Theorem was to be her greatest contribution to mathematics, but initially she was not credited for her breakthrough. When Germain wrote to Gauss she was still in her twenties, and, although she had gained a reputation in Paris, she feared that the great man would not take her seriously because of her gender. In order to protect herself, Germain resorted once again to her pseudonym, signing her letters as Monsieur Le Blanc.

—SIMON SINGH
Fermat's Enigma
Anchor Books, 1998

hit men named Vinnie, who suddenly start rigging explosives to your car's ignition system. I'm talking about subtle sabotage. Subtle sabotage means things like this:

- ☛ You relate some exciting news about your business to your husband, and he says, "Yeah, honey. That's great. Can ya bring me a beer?"

- ☛ You tell a good friend that you just got a big break: one of your most important prospects responded to your mischief marketing campaign and even made an appointment to see you. Your friend says, "Is that what you were wearing?" Or "You showed that crazy thing of yours to *him*?"

- ☛ You're struggling to meet an important deadline. Suddenly everybody wants you to help move furniture, mow lawns, baby-sit, go to parties, "stop working so hard," "have a little fun," and so on. Your answering machine goes bananas and starts dialing out by itself.

Similarly, whenever you embark on a mischief marketing campaign, expect resistance from the people closest to you. The sooner you learn about (and accept) this common phenomenon, the better off you'll be.

Friends love misery . . . . Sometimes, especially if we are too lucky or too successful or too pretty, our misery is the only thing that endears us to our friends.

—ERICA JONG
How to Save Your Own Life
Plume, 1995

And remember: these folks are not ignoring your achievements in order to hurt you. It's just that your marketing efforts don't fit their pictures of you, their preconceived notions about you. It confuses them about who you are. They've arranged the furniture of their minds so that you're a coffee table, and here you are suddenly turning into an ottoman. It mixes them up.

Sabotage from Acquaintances

Most human beings are naturally jealous and envious. In fact, if you want to know what most of us are really like underneath our carefully crafted, civilized exterior, visit a kindergarten. To paraphrase the title of a lovely book, everything you need to know about human nature you can learn from kindergarten.

This obvious fact is even reflected in language, specifically the language that religious leaders have used for centuries. They often address their parishioners or congregants collectively as "my children," or individually as "my child." They refer to people as children because it expresses the simple truth that most of us *are* like children.

Yet here is the problem that causes so much grief in the world: *we forgive children for being selfish, jealous, and envious, but we don't forgive adults.* If we recognized that most adults are actually children—something that genuinely spiritual people recognize—then we would not be so mad at the adults who offend us or obstruct our projects. We'd accept them for what they are—young children in old bodies.

Doing anything out of the ordinary will usually get someone on your case. You can't upset a child's routine, and these people are essentially spoiled children. If you get mad at them—and this applies equally to corporate boardrooms on Wall Street or in Silly/Con Valley—you hand them a victory. Your anger will allow them to distract you from pursuing your goal. You will become like a parent who can't go shopping because he or she doesn't know how to ignore a tantrum-throwing, spoiled child. No, the best thing to do with such "children" is to pay them no attention at all.

Sabotage from Your Prospect's Watchdogs

Another kind of sabotage comes from your prospect's professional watchdogs. Watchdogs are staff members who were hired to protect the boss from unwanted interruptions, unnecessary distractions, and crazy people like you.

One day, when you have finally arrived—when you've built your business into the next America Online, or when you've fulfilled your social or scientific mission—you, too, will need professional watchdogs. Why?

You will need watchdogs because what happens when you become successful is not what you think happens. It's not all about exciting parties, candlelit dinners, boardroom wizardry, or whatever scenarios you envision when you think of success. What really happens when you make it is that all sorts of people come crawling out of the woodwork to vie for your attention, while others become irrationally mad at you.

You need help to protect yourself from these characters, and your prospect is no different. That's why he or she has professional watchdogs

Mrs. Silliman

Whoopi's Friends Didn't Want to Party After All

*A*bout a year ago, a woman literally named Mrs. Silliman fought hard to stop one of her neighbors from running a home-based business. Silliman argued vehemently before her homeowners association and county zoning board that the neighbor's weekly total of two hours of piano instruction (what Silliman called her neighbor's "business") violated the rules of the housing subdivision in which they lived.

If you have a home-based business, how do you deal with neighbors like this? Do you ask their permission before you set up shop? What can you expect them to say if you do?

"The most encouraging thing your neighbors will usually say is, 'Oh, OK,'" says Rudy Lewis, president of the National Association of Home Based Businesses, a trade group in Owings Mills, Md. "But what they're really thinking is, 'Oh no, there goes the neighborhood!' I advise our members to be like the military policy on sexual preference: 'Don't ask; don't tell.' You let the neighbors know, and someone is always going to oppose you."

And such opposition can doom a home business. Neighborhood associations, growing more powerful, are enacting tighter rules to keep the lid on everything from dog droppings and repainting with the wrong color to home businesses that are perceived as interfering with communal tranquillity.

　—ROBERT JOHNSON
　"Battle on the Home Front"
　Wall Street Journal, April 19, 1999

*I*n an interview not long ago, Whoopi Goldberg mentioned how she always dreamed that when she finally made it, she would be able to take along all her friends from the old neighborhood and have wonderful parties and good times together with them. But it didn't turn out that way.

Whoopi didn't say why it didn't turn out that way, but she might easily have been thinking about the sabotage syndrome. For some strange, sad reason, when you start to do well, many of your friends will start saying, "Oh, so now you're too *good* for us, huh?" There is little you can do to stop them from alienating themselves from you in that way.

Idea Joggers

• Is there someone "above" you whom you resent for not answering your "requests"?
• Is there someone who you pretend is alienating you, when really it is you who are alienating yourself?

Don't I Know You from Somewhere?

M ichael Shurtleff has been the casting director for Broadway shows like "Chicago" and for films like *Jesus Christ Superstar* and *The Graduate*.

In his book, *Audition*, Shurtleff talks about how he got started in the business by writing a series of letters to the famous producer David Merrick. Although Shurtleff made it clear that he wanted to work for Merrick, the letters were conversational in tone. They talked about various items in the news, about dishy bits of gossip, and, above all, about Merrick's work. They were pithy, lively, and interesting. In fact, their focus was on Merrick and his shows, not on Michael Shurtleff.

Shurtleff's first letter to Merrick never got answered. Nor did his second, third, or fourth. In fact, none of his letters was answered. Yet every week, week after week, Shurtleff wrote another. After a while, he intensified his mischievous campaign and started sending two letters a week.

Finally, after about seven months, Merrick's secretary called Shurtleff to set up an appointment. Shurtleff was shocked, of course, but he was also delighted.

on staff. Often, these staff members are truly dedicated people who have known your prospect for many years and who really do have his or her best interests at heart. It's important for you, as a mischief marketer, to understand this. They may seem to be deliberately and spitefully getting in your way, but they are simply doing a necessary and important job.

The real question is how to distinguish between the two major types of watchdogs—the shepherds and the Chihuahuas.

The shepherds are the sincere, dedicated watchdogs we just talked about. They're the good guys.

The Chihuahuas, however, are the overzealous, somewhat stupid watchdogs who spastically bark at everything and everybody. They are the ones who will try to sabotage your marketing efforts. The tactic they most often use is to depict you as nothing more than a sycophant, a flake, a bad risk.

There will always be a person on your prospect's staff who hates you for adopting an unconventional or mischievous approach. This person probably spent years paying his or her dues, sucking up to the boss, going through proper channels, maybe embezzling a little on the side—and now despises himself or herself for having sold out so thoroughly. Naturally, the person will resent your skipping the safe, obsequious steps he or she took. They will see you as pulling a Get Out of Jail Free card. They will resent your freedom. And they will work very hard to sabotage you and your campaign. If you can't accept this fact, then you don't want to do mischief marketing.

When you conduct one of the gentler mischief marketing campaigns, you could appear to be fawning. And when you conduct one of the wilder campaigns, you could appear to be a flake. That's the bad news.

Cerberus

A grim, watchful keeper, house-porter, guardian, etc.

Cerberus, according to Roman mythology, is the three-headed dog that keeps the entrance of the infernal regions. Hercules dragged the monster to earth, and then let him go again.

Orpheus lulled Cerberus to sleep with his lyre; and the Sibyl, who conducted Æneas through the Inferno, also threw the dog into a profound sleep with a cake seasoned with poppies and honey.

The origin of the fable of Cerberus is from the custom of the ancient Egyptians of guarding graves with dogs.

—E. COBHAM BREWER
The Dictionary of Phrase and Fable
Harper and Row, 1970

They chatted in Merrick's office for two hours. Then, as the conversation wound down and Shurtleff started to leave, Merrick said casually, "Well, see you on Monday."

After all those letters, Shurtleff got the job.

The good news is that there are ways to correct that impression.

☞ Openly acknowledge what these people are probably thinking about you. Here's a good place to exercise the simple truth tactic. If you suspect your prospect is thinking that you're just kissing their butt, come right out and say so. Use humor. Say something like, "You must think I'm kissing your ass. Let me set you straight: I *am* kissing your ass." Then go on and make your pitch. In other words,

Don't Just Walk the Walk; Get a Carriage

*T*here's a story about two Orthodox Jewish men who are childless and very distressed about it.

Now, Orthodox Jews have a lot of faith in the efficacy of prayer, and they believe that in times of trouble you need to seek out the blessing of a holy man. So the two of them go together to visit a rebbe. They tell him what's wrong and ask him to beseech God for help. The rebbe grants their request and prays for them: "May God grant each of you a child within a year."

A year goes by. The first man's wife gets pregnant and gives birth to a baby boy. The second man and his wife remain childless, and he feels cheated. Why did the prayer work for the first guy, but not for him? He wants an answer to this question, so he storms back to the rebbe.

"Rebbe," he says, "this is very unfair of God. I don't see how I can place my whole faith in God when He treats me like this. You gave both of us the same blessing, and yet, while my friend now has a healthy baby boy, I have nothing.

acknowledge the truth about what people are thinking, then move on.

☛ Counterbalance your flattery. If you find yourself fawning (but sincerely!) over your prospect, step back for a moment and try something a little different. Like this: "Of course, I could be wrong about all this flattering stuff. Maybe you're not as great as I think you are. After all, I've never even met you. For all I know, you might actually be the biggest jerk in your field. In fact, many of your critics apparently think you're a dope. And maybe they're right. How would I know? But assuming that you really are the kind of person I think you are—then . . ."

If you fly it gracefully, this eye-catching kite can produce astonishing results. And notice that it's another variant on telling the simple truth.

Can you see how a lot of mischief marketing is really about spotlighting the truth? How it is not simply about cute little tricks?

Sabotage from Yourself

The fourth manifestation of the sabotage syndrome takes the form of self-sabotage. This is the most difficult one to deal with.

One way to sabotage yourself is by harboring an unconscious lack of faith. Do you really believe in yourself and your offering? If you do, you don't need to keep saying so. Instead, quietly do what you need to do in order to prepare for good things to happen. Don't just *say* you have faith in your offering. *Act* in faith. Or at least act *as though* you have faith. All the positive affirmations in the world mean nothing if you don't act on them.

Another way to sabotage yourself is by unconsciously trying to prove that someone has wronged you. In a court of law, the victim of a crime is asked to point out who wronged them. You see this depicted in movies all the time. At a climactic moment, in an atmosphere charged with tension, the victim on the witness stand rises, points dramatically at the defendant and declares, "It was him."

The defense attorney then says, "You mean it was *he*. Let the record reflect that the witness has bad grammar."

On a more serious note, be honest: if you fail at whatever you're trying to accomplish in business or in life, at whom will you feel entitled to point a finger and say, "I failed because of you?" Will it be your abusive mother or father? Your ex-husband or ex-wife? Your high school math teacher? Who will be proven the culprit if you fail? In what way will you get to be "right" when you point that accusing finger? Please. Forget about those people who treated you unfairly. There is no courtroom in which you'll be able to accuse them one fine day—at least not on this earth. That particular drama is all in your mind. We're all guilty of this vindication fantasy to some degree, so don't start pointing a finger at yourself, either.

On the other hand, if you *can* sue someone successfully—go right ahead. But don't sabotage yourself just to prove that someone else didn't treat you fairly—and turned you into a failure.

You might start by unconsciously undermining yourself because you can't stand the loneliness and the hard work involved in making your project work. This is another natural phenomenon. You find yourself sitting in a Red Clock Inn somewhere in Detroit. You're there because you have to be there to promote your business, but you hate it. You miss your family, your friends, your old life. So in the back of your mind, quietly, keeping it a secret even from yourself, you start thinking, "If I don't work so hard, my business will fail. Then I'll be able to

Tell me! What is the difference between me and my friend?"

"All right," the rebbe says. "If you insist, I'll tell you. The difference is this: After I gave you both the same blessing, you went home and waited, and your friend went out with his wife and bought a baby carriage."

go back to my old friends and my old life. I won't be lonely any more. I'll be back doing what's comfortable. Forget about starting a new life. It's too hard, too lonely."

Don't try to resist these "Why am I here?" ruminations. Repression gives them too much power. Neither resist nor succumb to them. Let them in, welcome them, and allow them to have their say; then get back to work. Plan for a time to revisit with your old life.

When I was writing this book, I thought for a while that it might be better to call this the sound barrier syndrome. Do you mind if I tell you why?

When aviation engineers first tried to break the sound barrier, they encountered lots of big and little difficulties. For instance, their airplanes would start to break up into pieces. That can be a real problem, you know.

But these engineers didn't take such problems personally. They didn't think, "Oh, Mother Nature hates us. She's trying to stop us from achieving our goals." They didn't think such things because they aren't true. Natural laws are not personal.

We remember this when we're talking about machines, but for some reason we forget it when we're talking about people. We sometimes think people are intentionally doing all sorts of things to sabotage us, but they're not. Oh sure, now and then you'll encounter a person with truly nefarious motivations. But it doesn't happen often. Most of the time, people simply are what they are, and they do what they do.

In fact, most of us are fairly mechanical. If you doubt that, try making yourself do something you hate, or something very difficult, something new. You'll quickly discover just how machinelike we all are. And this has nothing to do with your motivations. You could have the greatest motivations in the world, and still your machinelike nature will put up a barrier that stops you from accomplishing your objectives. Don't let it stop you.

I do not know why I do the things I do. I do not do what I want to do. But I do the things I hate.

—PAUL OF TARSUS

Dealing with Fear

This is a perfect opportunity to discuss another very important tactic: how to deal with your fear and how to distinguish between different kinds of fear.

All good mischief marketers experience fear when implementing their campaigns. After all, some of these techniques require you to be pretty bold. And if being bold doesn't come naturally to you (or even if it does), you're bound to get scared doing some of this stuff. But not all fear is the same. To be successful at mischief marketing, you need to learn to distinguish between panic and dread.

Panic Versus Dread

Think about nitroglycerine for a moment. As we all know, nitro is a very powerful explosive. Because it is so powerful, you might be tempted to think it would make a good fuel, but you'd be wrong. It makes a lousy fuel, because it's too volatile. You can't control nitro well enough to make it do anything useful. It can only explode destructively.

Hydrogen, on the other hand, makes a fantastic fuel because it burns cleanly and because it can be controlled. One day, our cars will probably run on hydrogen.

What does this have to do with the difference between panic and dread?

Panic is a bad kind of fear. It's a destructive force. It gets in your way. If panic were a fuel, it would be an unpredictable, unreliable fuel, like nitroglycerine. Dread, on the other hand, is a powerful, motivating force, and a good kind of fear. It is clean, concentrated, and controllable, like hydrogen.

You know that your mischief marketing is close to launch when you feel more dread than panic. The feeling of dread can be a signal that you're ready to go. It is a mix of excitement and anticipation, like that of a kid waiting to see Santa Claus for the first time.

So how do you tell the difference between panic and dread?

Panic is a high-pitched, nervous emotion. You're jumpy and confused when you're in a panic. Dread is a much lower-pitched, deeper, more profound, and more terrifying emotion. It may even be sickening. Ask any athlete or performer before a game or show. Dread is like stage fright, or pregame jitters. It's an adrenaline rush, certainly, but it's profoundly nauseating, too. When you look before you leap, it can sicken you, but you jump anyway.

Why dread is so unpleasant nobody really knows. Perhaps it's because, at the moment you experience authentic dread, you are standing at a crossroads in your life. Your fate, so to speak, is standing there beside you. In the human mind, fate and death are related.

Now, with regard to your fate (or the fate of your mischief marketing campaign) you can either choose it or refuse it. If you choose your fate, you'll move forward in your life. If you refuse it—well, you can't really refuse it, so let's put it this way: if you *try* to refuse it—you may get stalled. And if you get stalled, you may end up whining a lot, drinking, smoking, gambling, sleeping around, carping about other people's work, or generally just wasting time.

But that's okay. Maybe you need to stall a few times before you learn to take action in the face of dread. Nobody can blame you for doing so. This isn't easy stuff. If it were easy, everybody would be able to do it. It would be as easy as sitting on the couch munching chips and watching people scream at each other on the "Jerry Springer Show."

The bottom line is this: if you feel confused and nervous about your mischief marketing launch, then you're probably experiencing panic. In that case, here's a mischief marketing rule of thumb:

> If you're experiencing panic rather than dread, you may want to delay your campaign and spend some more time refining it. Panic is a yellow light (or even a red light). But if you feel either joy or dread about it, then you should probably give your project a green light.

Notice that last sentence. It says, "if you feel either joy or dread." Where did the "joy" come from? The answer is simple: joy is the flip side of dread. But that is beyond the scope of a book like this. Check mischiefmarketing.com for more.

Recognizing the Eleventh Hour Principle

I've talked about quite a few depressing things so far. I've discussed how trying to accomplish anything worthwhile will often leave you feeling abandoned and lonely; how other people will unconsciously try to sabotage your efforts; how you will unconsciously try to sabotage yourself; how your fears will hold you back; and how you may need to fail, and then turn your failures around.

So far, this doesn't seem much like a typical feel-good business book, does it?

Cheer up. Things will get better. But first I need to discuss two more obstacles you are likely to encounter in your mischievous travels: the eleventh hour principle and the ROT syndrome.

As noted in Chapter 7, the eleventh hour principle has to do with the fact that the darkest hour is just before dawn. This is not just a well-known cliché; it's the truth. The best things in life tend to come together only at the last minute. You plan, you work, you struggle, and yet, for the longest time, your efforts seem to be going nowhere. Then, all at once, things start falling into place, usually just when you're about to give up. If you don't understand the eleventh hour principle, you're likely to get depressed and surrender too soon.

> **Mischief Marketing Preparatory Tactic:**
>
> Remember the eleventh hour principle. Understand that it is when you are most depressed about your project or campaign that you are most likely to be nearing its successful completion.

Finding Your LORE

You may remember from physics that every electron has its own appropriate orbit. An electron that belongs in orbit 5, for example, cannot easily be forced into orbit 2, and vice versa. Well, a similar thing is true in marketing. A lot of us make the mistake of trying to market to the wrong prospects—people in the wrong orbit, so to speak. We usually assume, for instance, that we should always start small and market our offering only to our friends at first, or only to people in our hometown.

This philosophy works great—but only if that's the appropriate level at which you should be operating. It works very poorly if your appropriate level of recognizable effectiveness (LORE) happens to be, say, your entire home state instead of just your local town.

Imagine if Steve Jobs had tried to sell the original Apple computer only to people in his immediate neighborhood. Do you think he would have sold a lot of computers? Do you think he would have helped launch the personal computer revolution? Of course not. That local market did not embody his LORE. People on his block almost certainly would not have recognized the value of the personal computer at that time in history. His fledgling business would have flopped.

Are you having a hard time landing a job or getting your business off the ground? Then ask yourself: is it possible your LORE is not right for you? Is it possible your prospects can't recognize your level of effectiveness because you're thinking too small? Are your prospects in orbit 3, so to speak, while your offering belongs in orbit 5? If that's the case, no wonder you're struggling. If you try to operate at a level that's too low or too high for you, then you will surely run yourself up against a lot of brick walls.

The interesting thing about finding your LORE is that once you determine what it is, a filter-down effect comes into play. For instance, you might find that as soon as your offering is recognized at the state level, it starts getting recognized at the local level, too—the very level you couldn't make a dent in before. There's a trickle-*up* effect as well. Prospects at the national level, say, will observe that your offering works at the state and local levels, and they, too, will become interested in it.

So finding your correct LORE is vital. It will give you a position from which you can now target prospects both above and below your LORE, a position from which you can grow. A mischief marketer always tries to seek the correct level, the correct LORE for his or her offering. And how do you do that? It's simple. You shoot for the moon and work down from there until you find your place.

Think about pop culture genius Andy Warhol. By day, Warhol dressed like a slob so he could pretend to be working his way up from the bottom as a struggling artist. But by night, he went to society parties in his fancy Brooks Brothers clothes and made important social contacts. You gotta do both.

Don't assume it's better to operate at a higher level or that you're a superior person if you're able to do so. There are lots of dull-witted, untalented, dreadful people who quite naturally do very well at high levels on the heap. Remember the following two words, because they summarize this principle magnificently: Dan Quayle.

Mischief Marketing LORE Tip:

Start from the top and work down. Find your correct level of recognizable effectiveness.

So if discovering your LORE leads you to becoming president of General Motors, say, don't assume it means that you are in any sense better, or more capable or effective, than the president of your local pawnshop. It means nothing of the kind. All it means is that you found your appropriate level, your LORE.

When you try to go above that level, you will eventually rise to your level of incompetence and you'll find yourself in the territory of the famous Peter Principle.

Countering the Rejection of Old Truths (ROT) Syndrome

The truths in life that are hardest to grasp are the old, well-known truths. It's human nature to reject such ancient truths. We hear them and we say, "What a cliché," or "Oh, I already know that," or, "That's old guard." In other words, whatever our chronological age, we instantly become teenagers. We think we know it all.

Why are we like this? Well, one reason is that we live in a culture obsessed with newness. Everywhere you turn, people are screeching "It's New! New! New!" So whenever we encounter an old idea, we tend to dismiss it. Just as adolescents dismiss the wisdom of their parents, we dismiss the wisdom of our entire cultural heritage.

The ROT syndrome is incredibly powerful. In fact, it is so powerful that even if everyone were to wake up tomorrow and recognize the danger it poses, that recognition itself would become a well-known truth; then you and I would instantly dismiss the ROT syndrome, too, just as we dismiss every other well-known truth. In other words, the very identification of ROT would get co-opted by ROT itself.

Don't reject old truths just because they're old, and don't reject popular truths just because they're popular.

Mischievous Pop Quiz

1. In any field of endeavor, the
   essential difference between a
   professional and an amateur can be seen in the fact that the
   professional:
   a) makes more money.
   b) knows what can go wrong.
   c) plays golf.

2. Years ago, most people used to think that having cancer was a
   private matter because:
   a) most people are nuts.
   b) most people are totally fricking nuts.
   c) but they've figured out a way to validate each other's complete
   and utter madness.

3. The factors in mischief marketing that really matter are:
   a) tricks about how to break into movie studios.
   b) tricks about spilling perfume on department store floors.
   c) psychological and spiritual factors that affect your creativity.

4. The important thing to note in the story about the founders of
   Home Depot is that:
   a) they piled up empty boxes in order to make their warehouse
   look well stocked.
   b) they went through a period of rejection and abandonment.

5. Whenever you try to accomplish something important, the
   Gethsemane effect occurs because:
   a) people hate you personally and want to make you miserable.
   b) it's a natural phenomenon, like cold weather in winter.
   c) nobody loves you.

6. A good example of starting from the bottom and working your
   way up can be found in the history of:
   a) Blockbuster Video: Opened its first store with just one video
   b) Barnes & Noble: Started the chain with just one book
   c) Neil Armstrong: Got to the moon with just one step

THE THIRTEEN COMMANDMENTS OF MISCHIEF MARKETING

Now that you know most of the psychological and sociological pitfalls you're likely to encounter when you start mischief marketing, you're just about ready to get down to business. Your first task: to review the rules of the road.

I. Thou shalt not implement a mischief marketing strategy unless thou canst look upon thy work and say, yea, it is good; verily, I like it.

We've said this before, and we'll say it again: There is no point at all in doing mischief marketing unless your offering is superb. If you have a mediocre product, service, or idea, please forget about mischief marketing. It will actually work against you. It will look like you're trying to get attention for a stupid idea, and it will be true.

Mischief marketing works in part because of the contrast—sometimes shocking—between the oddity of the marketing technique and the excellence of the offering itself.

Think about it. Whenever you see something unusual happening, your first thought is usually, "Oh, this is weird [or funny, or whatever]." But in the back of your mind, you also think, "The person who did this must be a little weird, too." This sets up an expectation. You expect the person to be weird, maybe even nuts.

When it turns out that the person is *not* weird (and it had *better* turn out that way)—in other words, when it turns out that the person who did that oddball thing is actually intelligent and meticulous, and that she or he really has something good to offer—well, you're pleasantly sur-

BOWA Builders

When BOWA Builders got started back in 1987, the founders made sure their company stood out for its sheer excellence. For instance, while the competition was doing handwritten stuff, BOWA gave its customers proposals that looked great—in print, on letterhead, inside a folder with its logo on it.

They also used a little mischief marketing. When offering their remodeling services to people in a neighborhood in which the houses were nearly identical:

"One of our architects designed a flier that showed an image of a house that—just coincidentally—looked like those houses," [co-founder] Baker relates. *"You opened it up, and it showed the house renovated."*

—J. FINEGAN
"Bootstrapping: Great Companies Started with $1,000 or Less" *Inc.*, August 1995

By the way, although started with only $5,000, BOWA's revenues by 1994 had climbed to $1.7 million.

---

prised. The contrast between what you expected and what you got makes what you got look even better.

It's like what used to happen on the old "Candid Camera" TV show. When the victims of the show's prank realized that the whole production had been mounted for their benefit, that the entire situation had been meticulously orchestrated to elicit a response from them personally, they beamed. They loved it.

In the same delightful way that "Candid Camera" was confusing, a good mischief marketing campaign is confusing—at first. That very confusion is what creates a condition of receptiveness in your prospect for your message. When the confusion is followed by a high-quality message, the impact of that message is doubled. To put it in pseudomathematical terms:

Lowered expectations + high-quality offering = confusion.

Confusion = momentary receptivity.

Confusion creates a state of momentary receptivity? The short answer is yes. (The long answer is in books on Milton Erickson and psychology in general. For details, see the mischiefmarketing.com website.)

Have you ever gone to a movie thinking that it would be bad and later found yourself pleasantly surprised at how enjoyable it was? Well, that happened at least partly because your expectations were lowered. You were prepared to be more accepting and forgiving of the show. You did not go into the film saddled with lofty expectations or with anyone else's opinion to support or refute. You may first have thought it was just a "chick flick" for example, with nothing to offer you (except a chance to keep your date happy). And yet perhaps you came out astonished at how funny it was. Or vice versa: you may have expected it to be just a "dick flick," a dumb comedy/action film.

And yet perhaps you were moved in some personal and unexpected way. You were disarmed.

The mischief marketer seeks to disarm prospects with sudden excellence. Relieving them of their preconceptions, then pleasantly surprising them with a well-orchestrated, tailor-made reality—that's the job of the mischief marketing genius.

II. Thou shalt not irritate thy prospect.

My brother, Artie, had a gregarious, sunny, and mischievous personality. He was the kind of guy who could tease anybody and get away with it, even make you enjoy it. If Artie wanted to make fun of you, he knew just how far to go. He never crossed the line, never got offensive.

But he'd come close. There were days when I thought to myself, "If he says one more word about my being fat (or whatever he was teasing me about that day), I'm gonna deck him."

Yet he never said that word. He always knew precisely when to stop teasing. So instead of making me mad, he made me laugh. Artie knew how to do that with everyone. He brought a lot of fun into people's lives that way. He was a master kibitzer.

In a mischief marketing campaign, you need to be like that relative or that friend of yours (we all have one) who's a master kibitzer. You need to realize just how far to go with a joke. Nobody can teach you this. It's something you need to learn for yourself.

If you go too far with a mischievous strategy—even a wonderful strategy, a hilarious one—you'll irritate people or offend them. Then you'll need to go back and correct your mistake, which is a lot of extra work. So don't irritate people. Don't annoy them, don't hassle them, don't stalk them.

Sudden Excellence

Seventh Generation was doing very well selling things from its catalog. But at one point, founder Alan Newman starting thinking about the environmental impact of many of his company's products, especially holiday gifts. So he did something completely unexpected. He wrote what turned out to be a mischievous catalog editorial in which he urged his customer to buy less.

"It turned out to be one of the most brilliant marketing things I did—totally unintentionally," Mr. Newman says.

The novel editorial led to a flood of publicity in newspapers, magazines, and television talk shows, ensuring Seventh Generation's reputation as a new breed of socially responsible business. By 1990, annual sales had reached $6 million.

A ny good mischief marketing campaign will probably be offensive to someone. If you're afraid of being creative, you might as well abandon mischief marketing and go into a nice, respectable field where people are always trying to please all the people all the time—like politics.

Ben and Jerry weren't afraid to be creative. Soon after they launched their now-famous ice-cream business, they printed bumper stickers that said "Lick It." They left them on the store's counter and let customers take them for free.

It was a cute and effective promotion, but certain members of the local lesbian community took umbrage. Here's how Ben and Jerry invoked the spirit of mischief to handle the delicate situation:

Commonwoman, an alternative weekly newspaper, cited the bumper stickers as an example of offensive behavior in the local business community. Ben and Jerry responded by placing an ad in the newspaper that read as follows:

Despite the fact that Commonwoman *displayed our bumper sticker as an example of sexism in Burlington, and*

Despite the fact that Commonwoman *published an article advocating stealing from businesses, and*

Despite the fact that Commonwoman *disapproves of and threatens not to accept this ad because they fail to see the humor in it,*

Ben & Jerry's would like to thank Commonwoman *for its service to the community and would like to thank its*

many readers for supporting our store these many months.

—FRED LAGER
Ben and Jerry's: The Inside Scoop: How Two Real Guys Built a Business with a Social Conscience and a Sense of Humor
Crown Publishers, 1994

S oon after young P. T. Barnum landed a job in a general store, he traded a peddler some merchandise for a bunch of plain green bottles.

Barnum's boss was not happy about this, so Barnum promised to get rid of the bottles within three months—a feat so nearly miraculous that, today, it would be like pawning off a truckload of eight-track cassettes or copies of O. J. Simpson's book, *I Want to Kill You.* Barnum decided to try a wacky lottery.

This technique—although (to most people at the time) mischievous and amusing in Barnum's hands—has been extended too far. Telemarketers and mail-order peddlers have taken it well beyond mischief marketing into outright chicanery. In some modern (and inauthentic) versions of the technique, you don't even get a green bottle.

III. Thou shalt have fun.

You have no doubt gathered by now that mischief marketing is not just about marketing. It's about having fun while you go about your business.

In short, mischief marketing is about lightening up, enjoying life, and helping others to enjoy life, too. I know that sounds corny, but guess what? All the great truths in life are corny. All the positive, life-affirming truths are corny.

Sure, there are negative truths in life, too—about poverty, misery, war, death, disease, hypocrisy, and evil. These are death-affirming truths. They're certainly not corny.

The point is this: if you have both life-affirming truths and death-affirming truths before you, choose the life-affirming ones. Don't reject them just because they're corny. In a mischief marketing campaign, you want to communicate to your prospects that their association with you or your offering will make their lives better and brighter.

You want people to have fun, right? And the only way they can have fun is if you have fun. Having fun means living in the *process*, not in the result. If you study Zen archery, the masters will teach you that hitting the target is not the primary goal. The primary goal is to immerse yourself in the total physical, intellectual, and spiritual process that Zen Buddhism teaches—in this case through archery.

That's a hard concept for most of us to grasp because we're so competitive. When we hear someone say, "It's not the destination, it's the journey" we have a tendency to scoff. We think winning—hitting the target—is the most important thing. But it isn't. In fact, even if it were the most important thing, you would be more successful at winning if you stopped worrying about it and concentrated more on the process

A thousand tickets were offered at fifty cents each. Five hundred and fifty prizes were promised, and these ranged from twenty-five dollars to five dollars in goods, to be selected by the store's management.

"The tickets went like wildfire," Barnum said. "Customers did not stop to consider the nature of the prizes. Journeyman hatters, boss hatters, apprentice boys, and hat-trimming girls bought tickets. In ten days they were all sold."

The drawing was held. One out of every two tickets was a winner. The victorious customers crowded the store for their prizes of merchandise—and went away with green bottles. "Some of the customers were vexed," Barnum admitted, "but most of them laughed at the joke." And, miracle of miracles, in less than two weeks there were no more green bottles.

—IRVING WALLACE
The Fabulous Showman: The Life and Times of P. T. Barnum
Knopf, 1959

Yes, the World's Richest Human Used to Pick Through Garbage

Bill Gates and his friends turned the process of gathering information into an entertaining Salvation Army Mission Impossible.

Gates and his high-school friends pursued their intense interest in computers and programming to the extent of going through trash bins at a local computer company to find discarded programs. They retrieved papers from among the garbage, studied the operating systems and eventually wrote a report on the company's computer problems. The company hired them. While still a high-school senior, Vancouver, Washington–based software firm TRW hired Gates as a programmer.

—Who's Who in Finance and Industry 1996–97

than on the result. When you concentrate on the process, you have fun. Conversely, when you're having fun, it shows that you're concentrating on the process.

In our culture, the most powerful model we have available to us—the mythological structure underpinning our lives—comes from the world of business. Where the ancient Greeks had Zeus and Apollo, we have Alan Greenspan and Bill Gates. And you should see how *they* look wearing only a figleaf. You may deplore our modern devotion to money and business; you may wish we cared about something more obviously spiritual or soulful. But the fact is that business has supplanted most other forms of human endeavor for most people. It is, whether we like it or not, what inspires people.

When I say "business," I mean the business of entertainment, the business of medicine, and the business of sports, too. I mean every business. In every arena, the numinosity—the sense of value, awe, and mystery—that used to be associated with religious ideas has moved to business. Even when they mention Mother Teresa, for example, most writers and critics talk about what a great *business* wizard she was. They talk about how many jets she had, how much money she raised. When they mention the Catholic or the Mormon church, they immediately mention assets and holdings. These are the measures of our time.

But guess what? The golden calf is a great target for spiritual practice. You can make (out of the golden calf of business) a Zen target, a Christian target, a Jewish target, a Catholic target, a Mormon target, a New Age target. You name it. In short, you can use business to further your deepest spiritual development. You can do that because what matters is not the target, but the process; not winning, but how you play the game; not the destination, but the journey.

People have said this before, but nowhere is it as essential as it is in mischief marketing. If you're too grim and serious about making money (getting your hands on that golden calf), becoming a success, winning, or getting girls (or boys)—mischief marketing won't work for you. You simply won't be able to do it well. Your campaigns will have a fishy quality. They will stink. You'll be like a student of Zen archery who thinks only about hitting the target. You may hit the mark, but you'll miss the point.

If you take yourself too seriously, then· please: put your Wall Street suit back on, go to the bar, have another martini, and forget about it. Have you tried distributed accounting applications? That would be an exciting field for you.

The mischiefmarketing.com website talks about something called the Humor Project. It offers scientific studies on the beneficial effects of humor and practical suggestions for weaving humor into the fabric of your life.

Humor is the good natured side of a truth.

—MARK TWAIN
Quoted in *Mark Twain and I*
Opie Percival Read
Folcroft Library Editions, 1973

IV. Thou shalt not bear false witness for thine offering.

In other words, don't lie.

When you read about the Vulcan tactic in Chapter 12, you'll learn that, although you should never lie about your offering, you can and should allow people to draw whatever favorable conclusions they want to draw about you. But there is another form of lying that you may not be aware of. And the chances are pretty good that, if you're reading this kind of book, you're probably already lying in just the way I'm about to describe. In fact, you may have been lying like this, perhaps without realizing it, for years.

I'm talking about *lying down*—and yes, the pun is intended. I don't mean lying up, aggrandizing your offering, but lying down. Lying down means making your offering appear less than what it really is, putting yourself down so that you can seem more humble and more of a nice

Mischief
Marketing
or Hairy
Deception?

According to the Bible, Isaac was the father of Jacob and Esau. When Isaac was old and lay dying and nearly blind, he called his older son, Esau, over to him and promised to bless him. But he first wanted Esau to hunt down some wild game and "Prepare me the kind of tasty food I like and bring it to me to eat, so that I may give you my blessing before I die."

The young men's mother, Rebekah, overheard this conversation. So while Esau was off hunting, she told Jacob to "Go out to the flock and bring me two choice young goats, so I can prepare some tasty food for your father, just the way he likes it. Then take it to your father to eat, so that he may give you his blessing before he dies."

Jacob was nervous about carrying out this bit of mischief. He said: "But my brother Esau is a hairy man, and I'm a man with smooth skin. What if my father touches me? I would appear to be tricking him and would bring down a curse on myself rather than a blessing." His mother replied: "My son, let the

person. But remember: "Give credit where credit is due" is a saying that applies to yourself as much as it does to anyone else. Be objective. If your offering is good, don't be afraid to say it. There will always be someone who is more than willing to point out your flaws. If you make this person's job any easier, you'll take all the fun out of it for him or her.

If you keep lying down, people will eventually believe you, and your lie may never be discovered. Consequently, you will miss all kinds of sparkling opportunities and eventually end up a victim of your own humility.

You know what's really amazing about all this? Your prospects *want* to believe the best of you! They don't want to know all your flaws. They don't want to eat all your humble pie. They want to believe your offering is wonderful; they want you to teach them whatever it is they'd like to learn; they want to enjoy whatever product or service you're offering. When you're lying down—telling them all the things that are wrong with you, refusing to let them believe what they want to believe, you disappoint people. You cheat them out of what they want.

Here's another thing: your prospects want to be the ones who discovered you first. That's a rare distinction. Think of the producers who gave the crew at "Saturday Night Live" their first break. Don't you think they're proud of that? Who wouldn't love to say, "I gave Steven Spielberg his

And the Devil did grin, for his darling sin Is pride that apes humility.

—SAMUEL TAYLOR COLERIDGE AND ROBERT SOUTHEY "The Devil's Thoughts" first directing job,"or "I was one of the original venture capitalists who launched Netscape"?

Does this mean that you should go around bragging all the time? Certainly not. It simply means that in a mischief marketing campaign, you never lie about your offering. You don't lie up, and you don't lie down. You don't lie, period.

V. Thou shalt be humble and honest.

We just finished saying you shouldn't lie down about your offering or yourself, and now we're saying you should be humble and honest. If there appears to be a contradiction here, it's because this whole mischief marketing process is a tightrope act, one of those things in life that require you to strike a delicate balance between two apparently opposing principles.

In mischief marketing, to be humble means to acknowledge your limitations, but it also means to refrain from advertising your shortcomings.

Knowing the right time to admit your faults is almost an art in itself. The right time is usually when someone asks you an embarrassing question—which you then answer honestly without hesitation. There is even a right time to advertise your flaws.

The famous advertising slogan that said, "With a name like Smucker's, it has to be good" is an excellent illustration of when and how to be humble in the marketplace of ideas. It was a very successful ad campaign because it was humble and honest. It worked because it also dragged out into the open—boldly—something that people happened to be thinking anyway. After all, Smucker's really is a strikingly odd name. For the company to come right out and admit that truth about what people were thinking was downright refreshing.

curse fall on me. Just do what I say." Which he did.

Then Rebekah found Esau's best clothes, put them on Jacob, covered his hands and neck with goatskins, and handed Jacob the food she had made.

Here, according to the New International Version, is the rest of the story:

He went to his father and said, "My father." "Yes, my son," he answered. "Who is it?"

Jacob said to his father, "I am Esau your firstborn. I have done as you told me. Please sit up and eat some of my game so that you may give me your blessing." Isaac asked his son, "How did you find it so quickly, my son?" "The Lord your God gave me success," he replied. Then Isaac said to Jacob, "Come near so I can touch you, my son, to know whether you really are my son Esau or not."

Jacob went close to his father Isaac, who touched him and said, "The voice is the voice of Jacob, but the hands are the hands of Esau." He did not recognize him, for his hands were hairy like those of his brother Esau; so he blessed him.

—GENESIS 27:1–23

> ## Mischief Marketing Tip:
>
> In the marketplace of products and ideas, honesty and humility are powerful forces when they confront and expose things that people are already thinking.

In judo, you use your opponent's energy to propel his or her body in the direction in which it is already moving, thereby cutting your own energy expenditure in half. Professional stand-up comics know this principle very well. If you want to be a stand-up comic but you happen to be fat or skinny, or you have a big nose, crooked teeth, or a kooky voice—in short, if there's anything unusual about you that everyone notices immediately—then you'd better acknowledge that fact as soon as possible. With that out of the way, you can move on to the business at hand. If you don't do that, the audience won't listen to you, and they won't think you're funny. In the business arena, you'll lose credibility in the eyes of your prospect.

> ## Mischief Marketing Tactic:
>
> The Liberace Gambit—If there's something strange or unusual about you or your offering, don't cover it up—*play* it up.

Stand-up comedy, by the way, can be a great training ground for mischief marketing. A little later, we'll talk about why that's true.

Of course, whenever you're honest, you also incur the risk that people will make fun of you. For instance, "Saturday Night Live" once did a skit on the Smucker's slogan that featured ridiculous names for jam such as Nose Hair, Death Camp, Mangled Baby Ducks, Dog Vomit, Monkey Pus, and Painful Rectal Itch. Smucker's got free advertising out of that hilarious sketch. So even if people do poke fun at you for being honest—or for any reason—it can, in the long run, work in your favor.

VI. Thou shalt make thine execution of a mischief marketing strategy elegant and flawless.

This is related to but different from the first commandment, which says that your offering must be superb. More than that, *every* element of your campaign, not only the offering itself, must look, sound, feel, and be impeccable.

For example, let's suppose you're a very young scientist who has discovered a cure for cancer using computer simulation software. You want to bring your work to the attention of the editors of the scientific journal *Nature*, but you know they won't pay a whiff of attention to you because you're only fifteen years old. (In case you think this example is too far-fetched, note that the famous physicist Blaise Pascal was only eleven when—in order to get around his father's strict ban on reading books about mathematics—he constructed a geometry of his own.)

Working with what resources you have at your disposal as an ambitious fifteen year old, you decide to launch a polite but persistent letter-writing campaign to the editors of Nature. (This strategy is discussed in the story about Michael Shurtleff in Chapter 8; it's a tried and true technique.) Every week you write your mischievous letter. Unfortunately, you use cheap paper ripped out of a notebook, your handwriting stinks, and you make a lot of spelling mistakes.

Is it good to be sloppy about your otherwise excellent letters? Of course not. You already have one strike against you—the fact that you're fifteen years old. If you're sloppy and careless on top of that, you'll have two strikes against you.

Even if your mischievous campaign is based on the humorous idea of letters from a kid who thinks he has a cure for cancer, you still need to make your communications look good, perhaps with beautiful paper, magnificent envelopes, or lovely packaging. It's similar to what they teach acting students: if you're playing a character who is bored, you can *act* bored but you cannot *literally* bore the audience.

A Word About Kamikaze Marketing

Some unfortunate souls who try to do mischief marketing violate the sixth commandment and end up doing kamikaze marketing instead. They try to get attention by stalking people, sending dead insects in the mail, and so on. (Yes, there are a lot of people who do this.)

One key factor that distinguishes a kamikaze from an authentic mischief marketer is that a kamikaze is always cheap. A kamikaze will never spend a few extra dollars on a beautiful package, for example. No, he or she will always go with basic, ugly, Ted Kaczynski brown paper wrapping, and the efforts will therefore bomb. You don't want to send ugly things in the mail; you don't want to misspell anything; you don't want to be sloppy, careless, rushed, cheesy, chintzy, crummy, sleazy, or dirty.

Let me tell you the secret that has led me to my goal.
My strength lies solely in my tenacity.

—LOUIS PASTEUR
Quoted in the *Barnes and Noble*
Book of Quotations, 1987

You need to signal to your prospects, in other words, that you know what you're doing despite the fact that you don't fit their conventional mold. You want them to know you are someone who has good taste and good judgment; an interesting someone who might be communicating humorously or mischievously but is doing so with craftsmanship (craftily, if you will), someone whose offering is worth a look, if only to satisfy their curiosity.

In a mischief marketing campaign—no matter how bizarre or silly its core theme—you want to look your best. You don't want anything to detract from your offering or taint it in any way.

Consider a fashion model who is dressed to the nines and looks stunning. Hair's all done up, makeup's perfect, lovely new dress, matching shoes and purse—and a glaring run in her hose. The whole image she wanted to create is destroyed by that single flaw. It's not that she herself isn't the vision of beauty she wanted to be, but all you will remember of her is that she had that run in her hose.

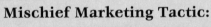

Mischief Marketing Tactic:

If you're sure how to make it flashy and perfect, keep it casual, simple—and perfect.

VII. Know well the rules before thou breakest them.

James Joyce once wrote a book called *Finnegans Wake* in which he broke nearly every rule of writing.

Had Catholic nuns been present in Joyce's home during the composition of this book, they would no doubt have beaten him into a coma with a yardstick. On the following page is a sample passage from that book.

 First, thou shalt not smile. Twice thou shalt not love. Lust, thou shalt not commix idolatry. Hip confiners help compunction. Never park your brief stays in the men's convenience. Never clean your buttoncups with your dirty pair of sassers. Never ask his first person where's your quickest cut to our last place. Never let the promising hand usemake free of your oncemaid sacral. . . . Never dip in the ern while you've browsers on your suite. Never slip the silver key through your gate of golden age. Collide with man, collude with money. Ere you sail foreget my prize. Where you truss be circumspicious and look before you leak, dears.

—JAMES JOYCE
Finnegans Wake

What the hell does this passage mean? Who knows. Only eleven people in the world understand *Finnegans Wake*, among them my friend Stephen in Staten Island (but, sadly, nobody understands them either). Many readers of Joyce get stuck simply trying to decipher why there's no apostrophe in *Finnegans*. It is said—and I have no reason to doubt it—that some literary scholars, after years of laboriously trying to crack the code, dump all their possessions into shopping carts and wander around Manhattan shrieking obscenities.

But as you can see from the selection, James Joyce did some extraordinary things. He shuffled clauses, twisted sentences, made up new words, mixed old words together, packed all sorts of different ideas and shades of meaning into a tight space, and transformed English literature in the process. *Finnegans Wake* violated many rules about writing. That's what made it outstanding.

Joyce was able to break the rules in a way that was brilliant and masterful. Because he knew those rules so well, he could break them elegantly, precisely, and artfully. He was an acrobat, an Olympic gymnast of language.

If you don't believe it, read the passage several times. After a while, it will begin to make sense, like one of those 3-D pictures you have to stare at for a few minutes before you can see the encoded image. You want to make people stare deeply at your offering. To create that kind of depth, to break out of two dimensions into three, you have to know lots of rules about vision.

It's like this: you can put together a new engine by mixing and matching odd parts from different engines, but you can't just slap *any* old parts together like so many Tinkertoys. You have to understand enough about engines to know exactly how to put a new one together so it will work; otherwise, you'll end up with a motor that is an inert . . . sculpture, maybe? In other words, you need to be a master mechanic. You need to have mastered the rules before you can break them—and still come up with a working engine.

The same is true in mischief marketing. Let's take an example.

Suppose you've decided you're going to break some of the accepted rules about writing and marketing a Hollywood screenplay. The first thing you need to study is exactly what those rules are. And if you've ever studied that particular subject, you know that Hollywood has a lot of amazingly complicated rules about screenplays. Some of these are unspoken rules, even insider rules.

Screenplays for Hollywood need to feature a certain amount of sex, for example; the dialogue needs to include a certain amount of wise-cracking banter; a certain number of objects need to be blown up; and so on. And that's just for starters. If you want to break these rules, you need to know what they are, how they work, and how you can twist them to create an interesting inflection. By knowing these rules, you have a chance—a slim chance, but a chance nevertheless—of camouflaging what you're *really* trying to do in your movie so that it closely resembles what Hollywood people are accustomed to seeing in a screenplay. You have a chance of slipping in under their radar.

Even Shakespeare did this sort of thing. Yes, the king of the English language used pop devices, too. Have you ever noticed all the silliness that goes on in a Shakespearean play? Most of it isn't funny to audiences today, but Shakespeare did not put it in there for today's audiences. He put that stuff in his plays for the people living in *his* time. And he needed to do that so that he could smuggle his *real* stuff under his audience's bawdy radar. Bawdy. They always use that word in connection with Shakespeare's audiences. Makes you think of bumpy-nosed people who had not made much progress in the field of cosmetic dentistry. But never mind that.

To summarize, there are two good reasons for knowing the rules in any given field before you break them: (1) to demonstrate that you're smart enough to have mastered those rules; and (2) to be able to use the rules to generate a kind of camouflage—a reasonably conventional outer appearance—so that the uniqueness of your offering won't immediately be rejected, as a healthy donated heart might be rejected by the recipient's body if the cardiologist didn't know how to use immunosuppressant drugs.

VIII. Thou shalt take risks.

Think about the first person who ever made a loaf of bread.

This person must have sat down and said something like: "Hmmm. Let me take these here wheat grains. Okay. Now, I think I'll soak them and then dry them out. Now what? Hmmm. Well, why not pummel them into a fine powder with this rock? Okay. Now I'll throw in some water. And what's this weird fungus-type thing over here? Let's call it—yeast; why not. Yeah, I'll throw some of that in, too. Okay. Now what should I do? I know: I'll stick the whole thing in the fire. Oh, look. Wow. It's puffing up like it's alive or something. You know what? I think I'll eat it. I hope it doesn't kill me."

Now *that* was a person who knew how to take risks.

To conduct a successful mischief marketing campaign, you have to think like the first person who ever made a loaf of bread. You have to combine unusual elements together; you have to think in new ways; you have to experiment; you have to be fearless. Picture a toddler walking across the kitchen floor for the first time. That's how fearless you need to be. You have to move past your nervousness and get on with whatever it is you would dare to do.

The good news is that no matter what risks you may need to take in order to conduct a successful mischief marketing campaign, your chances of achieving your goal, statistically speaking, are literally hundreds, perhaps thousands, of times greater than your chances of winning a lottery. The next time you go to a store and watch people scratching off lottery tickets, remember this statistical detail. It's an enormously effective visualization exercise that can keep you on track.

IX. Thou shalt learn how to fail and never to give up.

For many years, Babe Ruth held the world's record for home runs. At the same time, he held the world's record for strikeouts. The lesson people always extract from this oft-cited fact is that in order to be successful at something, you need to be willing to go to bat—and strike out time and time again.

It is hilariously simple, yet its very simplicity is what makes it so hard to grasp.

In the classic film *The Wizard of Oz* the good witch tells Dorothy that all she has to do to return home to Kansas is click the heels of her ruby slippers together. Dorothy, a little peeved, says something like, "Why didn't you tell me that before?" The good witch replies, with infuriating sweetness, "Because you wouldn't have believed me."

We are all failures—at least, all the best of us are.

—J. M. BARRI
Rectorial Address
St. Andrew's University, Scotland
May 3, 1922

Our doubts are traitors, and make us lose the good we oft might win by fearing to attempt.

—WILLIAM SHAKESPEARE
Measure for Measure
Act 1, Scene 4

Forget about mischief marketing. Forget every theory you've ever heard about marketing, gardening, fishing, pitching, writing, or exercising; every theory about making music, art, love, or money. Forget it all. The only thing you really need to know about how to be good at anything in the world is this: never give up.

Relax, take a break, but never give up. Meditate, pray, hand over your sorrows to a higher power. But never give up. Fail once, twice, three times, fifty times. But never give up. Get used to failing. Learn to love it, or hate it. Get sick and tired of trying again and again, or try something else. But never give up. Try a new approach, have a bout of depression, try another new approach, have another bout of depression, lose your enthusiasm, get mad, scream, "I can't take it anymore!" But never give up. Let people make fun of how often you keep trying. But never give up.

If you want help with this, listen to the music of Beethoven. (Get a recording by a good conductor, not a cheesy version by the Slobovian National Restroom Orchestra, on sale for $2.99.) Beethoven is one of the most tenacious composers in history. Listen to his Third, Fifth, and Ninth Symphonies, keeping in mind that this is the music of a deaf man, much of it. Now honestly: if a deaf man can make such brilliant music, can't you succeed at what you're trying to accomplish in your business or in your life? Of course you can. You just need to know how not to give up. Beethoven will show you how.

If anyone has conducted a Beethoven performance, and then doesn't have to go to an osteopath, then there's something wrong.

—SIMON RATTLE
The Guardian, May 31, 1990

Nothing in the world can take the place of persistence. Talent will not; nothing is more common than unsuccessful men with talent. Genius will not; unrewarded genius is almost a proverb. Education alone will not; the world is full of educated derelicts. Persistence and determination alone are omnipotent.

—CALVIN COOLIDGE

How could they tell?

—DOROTHY PARKER
Upon hearing of the death of "Silent" Calvin Coolidge

So please, if you get nothing else out of this book, rip out these pages and stick them up on your wall. They're the most important pages in the entire book.

If you want to read a great story about not giving up even after you've failed miserably—a story about how to turn your failures the way a martial arts master flips an opponent—check out the story of Ralph Hayles in Chapter 14.

X. Thou shalt not be a phony rebel.

Remember John Hinckley? He was the crazy guy who tried to win the heart of Jodie Foster by shooting President Reagan. We can either laugh or cringe (or both) at the logic of someone like this. But the truth is that sometimes, in our own lives, we do much the same thing.

Many of us are natural mischief marketers. We just don't know it yet. But instead of applying our mischievous talents to good goals, we apply them to bad goals—without meaning to. This is called inauthentic (phony) mischief marketing.

You see, by shooting the president, John Hinckley was trying to impress Jodie Foster with his bravery. That seems ridiculous to most of

Hall's Barbecue Sauce

When Tim Hall and his dad started a barbecue sauce business (Hall's Specialty Foods), their recipe had already won top awards in several statewide cooking contests, including the prestigious California State Fair. So they knew it was good stuff. Superior quality was not the problem.

The problem was whether they could sell it in large enough quantities to make a living from the business (gourmet food is a tough field), and whether they could charge the premium price they'd have to set for such a high-quality product.

One day they got a big break: an appointment to meet one of the buyers for the huge Costco chain. The buyer took one look at their proposal and said, "Who would want to spend so much money for barbecue sauce? Why, just this morning I had a meeting with a guy who was selling a barbecue sauce for 20 percent less than yours. Why should I buy your sauce? Why should I spend 20 percent more for a product nobody ever heard of?"

Tim said nothing because he had brought along a sales professional who told him to keep quiet during the meeting. Now came the time for the pro to do his job. He showed the buyer charts, numbers, and projections. He talked about the market; he used psychology; he used every selling tool in his arsenal to try to persuade that buyer to give them the account. He was an excellent salesperson, but the buyer was unmoved. He'd heard it all before. He just couldn't see why this sauce deserved a premium price.

Finally, Tim spoke up. Instantly, the sales pro shot him a glance because Tim wasn't supposed to say anything. But Tim couldn't sit around and watch his dad's offering get drowned in a sea of sales chatter. "Do you have that bottle of sauce my competitor brought to you earlier?" Tim asked. "Yes," said the buyer. "Then would you mind going to get it, along with two small paper cups?"

A minute later, the buyer was back with the competing sauce and the paper cups. Tim poured the cheaper sauce into one of the cups. "You see how watery this sauce is? It's like ketchup." The buyer nodded.

Then Tim took his dad's sauce and poured it into the other cup. "Now—you see how much thicker our sauce is? Look at these big, juicy chunks of pineapple. Look at how slowly the sauce eases out of the bottle. Taste it. Taste both of them." The buyer did, and they got the account.

Such is the power of one of the most mischievous marketing tactics in the world—telling the simple truth.

us. We look down on a guy like that, and we judge him—and rightly. He was being inauthentically mischievous. He was nuts.

But do we really have the right to judge him? Admit it: isn't what Hinckley did really just an exaggerated version of what a lot of us do, or have done? How many of us, for example, have engaged in supposedly daring acts that were secretly meant only to impress someone (or ourselves) with our stamina? Oh, we may not have tried to shoot the president, but how many of us have tried to act "brave" by consuming dangerous quantities of alcohol, for instance? Or drugs? Or by making life hard for ourselves? Is this really so different from what Hinckley did? Sure, it's different in degree, but not in kind.

When you do *authentic* mischief marketing, you must be willing to search your soul to discover the difference between authentic and inauthentic mischief marketing. Don't be mischievous just for the sake of being mischievous. Don't be rebellious just to show off. That's kid's stuff at best, and crazy at worst. Instead, walk the tightrope. Find the right balance between being too bold on the one hand and too timid on the other. And do it for yourself, because you always wanted to.

It's like being on a first date. Should you be bold or gentle? Should you be silly or serious? Quiet and cryptic, or talkative and open? Nobody can make these decisions for you. All of life—in business, art, politics, or marketing—is a courtship with humankind. In mischief marketing, as in love and life, you need to be honest and real.

XI. Thou shalt know thy prospect well.

In an earlier chapter, we talked about learning as much as possible about your prospects—"profiling"

The Big Rock of Power vs. the Little Rock of Truth

*I*n 1954, for the first time in the nation's history, the Supreme Court ruled that blacks could go to all-white schools. So in 1957, when nine black students tried to attend Central High School in Little Rock, Arkansas, white racists fluttered in from all over the South to stop them. But the events that followed were recorded by unblinking television cameras that "simply" broadcast the evils of discrimination to the world, and to history.

As the Arkansas National Guard tried to stop the kids from going to school, the television cameras simply rolled. As white mobs mocked and pushed and screamed at the kids, the television cameras simply rolled. As one thousand paratroopers from the 101st Airborne platoon, sent by President Eisenhower, marched down the street to protect the students, flanking them, as though folding them under the wings of the United States Constitution itself, the television cameras simply rolled.

The TV commentators didn't say much. They didn't

(continued)

have to. The simple truth spoke volumes for them. All they had to do—and it was an *extremely* mischievous thing for television to do in 1957—was "simply" keep those cameras going. Here is how one commentator put it:

> In a story of this moral intensity, John Chancellor and [TV reporters like him] were, in fact, modern day prophets. And he might as well be saying, while the camera is rolling, "This is a sin. This is a sin. This is a sin."

—DAVID HALBERSTAM

*E*ven in science, if you want to get across a fundamental truth, you sometimes need to penetrate through a thicket of confusion. One classic way to accomplish that is with parody.

> Sokal, a physicist at New York University, caused an intellectual row . . . when he fooled the editors of a modish academic journal called Social Text into publishing a sham article he had written. Bearing the title "Transgressing the Boundaries: Toward a

them the way an FBI psychologist might. We learned, for instance, that people who are famous for running corporations are usually prouder of how they cook lasagna (or play golf, sing, write poetry, bowl, play cards, or whatever) than they are of how they make the big business deals for which they're so well known.

We also learned how to apply this odd fact about human nature to the process of crafting a precisely targeted mischief marketing campaign that will help you win the attention of such a prospect. But that's for later.

Mischief Marketing Tip:

The more you can learn about your prospect, the better your chances will be.

Get inside your prospect's mind, see the world from her point of view, walk her walk, and talk her talk. The more you can do these things, and do them without sacrificing your own identity or your own principles, the more potent your mischief marketing efforts will be. Find similarities between you and your prospect. Use those to relate to your prospect. If you do this thoroughly and genuinely, why, all the better to see her, my dear.

XII. Remember the power of the simple truth.

Sometimes, the most mischievous thing in the world you can do is tell the truth. The story of Hall's barbecue sauce illustrates this in a way that doesn't require much explanation.

If you really want to know something about the power of the simple truth in the mischief marketing of important social or political ideas, watch a video about the civil rights movement.

 XIII. If thou perpetratest a hoax, thou shalt reveal it as such thyself.

Enough said.

The Commandments in Action

Let's talk about the comedic activism of a guy who illustrates quite well how these commandments work in practice—Michael Moore.

Filmmaker, journalist, and television star Michael Moore is a genius at mischief marketing. True, he's also a card-carrying liberal, which means that he tends to hold the same opinions as most of his liberal colleagues. But he's a mischief marketing genius nevertheless. Moore is best known for his satirical documentary, *Roger & Me*, for his award-winning television series, "TV Nation," and for the newer series, "The Awful Truth." Specializing in defending the economically and politically downtrodden, Moore's hilarious approach to political and social activism—the marketing of ideas—has attracted critical accolades and legions of fans.

If you really want to know how to do mischief marketing, and specifically how to use comedy as a weapon in the service of social reform, watch one of Michael Moore's films or TV shows. And as you're watching them, notice how Moore fulfills nearly all the mischief marketing commandments. You may not always agree with his ideas, but he does present them mischievously well.

Here are examples for each commandment.

Transformative Hermeneutics of Quantum Gravity," the article was meant to be a parody of what is loosely called post-modernist thought. It was crammed full of meaningless references to esoteric ideas in mathematics and physics, from which it leapt, in one breathtaking non sequitur after another, to radical conclusions about politics and society. . . .

It was a good joke. . . . But Sokal was up to more than mischief. The purpose of his hoax, he declared, was to reveal the fraudulence of much post-modernist thought, especially as it abused science.

—JIM HOLT
"Is Paris Kidding?"
New York Times,
November 15, 1998

1. Thou shalt not implement a mischief marketing strategy unless thou canst look upon thy work and say, yea, it is good; verily, I like it.

Moore's offering is almost always superb. He usually addresses real problems involving real people. For instance, he once successfully (and hilariously) embarrassed a tightfisted health care company into granting one of its policyholders the money to get a life-saving pancreas transplant.

2. Thou shalt not irritate thy prospect.

Moore never irritates his prospects. Oh, he irritates *other* people, all right, but not his prospects—who are the members of the viewing public enjoying his show or film.

The people he does annoy, and very amusingly, are politicians, bureaucrats, and corporate fat cats who collect millions of dollars in unearned compensation and bonuses while cheating or otherwise abusing hundreds of thousands of people (us). These are often the same folks, by the way, who huffily criticize the gambling industry—while they themselves gamble daily with our livelihoods, and even our lives.

3. Thou shalt have fun.

Moore always has a good time. During the Clinton impeachment craze, he carted a bunch of "Puritans" in full period dress to the Capitol and had them enact a frenzied, realistic, Salem-style witch-hunt complete with hysterical screaming, fainting, and rolling around in hallways outside the politicians' offices.

4. Thou shalt not bear false witness for thine offering.

Moore never lies about what he's doing. It is always clear that he's doing comedy. Scathing, biting comedy, yes; but comedy nevertheless.

5. Thou shalt be humble and honest.

Moore doesn't always exemplify this particular commandment, so I'll just skip over it.

6. Thou shalt make thine execution of a mischief marketing strategy elegant and flawless.

Moore's production values are often excellent. He sometimes goes all out with lighting, sound, casting, staging, costuming, editing, and musical scoring. In the case in which he helped the pancreas patient, Moore printed up colorful invitations to the man's supposedly impending funeral and presented them to many people, including the insurance company bureaucrat who didn't want to help the dying man get his transplant. (The company did relent, eventually. It now covers all such cases.)

7. Know well the rules before thou breakest them.

Moore knows the rules about television and video reporting. He also knows how to sell his offering to producers. He has excellent sales skills, rare for someone marketing moral values.

If you're marketing moral values, there's a myth that you're supposed to be naive, poverty-stricken, and weak. But of course if you actually *are* naive, poverty-stricken, and weak, you can't market much of anything, can you? What a marvelous double bind. Greatest invention of evil Mammon since slavery.

8. Thou shalt take risks.

Moore takes big risks. He regularly brings his cameras into places where people try to throw him out. In some cases, you can tell they'd probably bash his skull in if only the cameras weren't rolling.

9. Thou shalt learn how to fail and never to give up.

Moore never gives up. He relentlessly pursues the victims of his embarrassing exposés. He follows them into their offices and into elevators. He's gentle, but relentless.

10. Thou shalt not be a phony rebel.

Moore is not a phony rebel. He doesn't do destructive things. He doesn't shoot innocent people in abortion clinics. He doesn't complain about the world with his ass perched on a barstool. He doesn't send explosives through the mail. He doesn't eviscerate the credibility of a good cause by posing as an extremist proponent of it. He doesn't try to trick senior citizens into buying dozens of magazines so they can win ten million dollars. He communicates with humor, grace, and real power.

11. Thou shalt know thy prospect well.

Moore is essentially a journalist. He does background investigations of the corporations and individuals he exposes. He cites statistics and even conducts polls. They are often frivolous polls, but polls nevertheless.

12. Remember the power of the simple truth.

Moore's camera is an unblinking eye that records the simple truth. He never attacks people viciously. He just allows them to reveal who they really are—on film, in front of millions of people.

13. If thou perpetratest a hoax, thou shalt reveal it as such thyself.

When Moore perpetratestetheths a hoax, he doth revealeth it as such hisself.

In Summary

Michael Moore's mischievous campaigns are not what you'd call subtle, but they are often brilliant and entertaining. In your own business, you may want to do something less wacky, but the blueprint is there for you in his work. Take the best and discard the rest.

I'll close this chapter with a few thoughts on mischief marketing and political perspective.

To Readers Who Lean Toward the Right or Toward Libertarianism

The preceding discussion singing the praises of Michael Moore could easily mislead some folks into thinking that mischief marketing is a leftist, commie, big government, do-gooder enterprise. It is not. Mischief marketing is a business tool. Like any other business tool, it can be used for good or evil. That the author happens to share Moore's distaste for corporate abuse has nothing to do with the effectiveness of the techniques in this book. Even if you're a *laissez-faire,* libertarian capitalist, I'm sure you can agree that what mischief marketers like Moore are doing is preferable to letting the government enact misguided legislation that chokes the market.

Humor is a knife that cuts both ways, so even if you are a corporate fat-cat abuser of the working class, you can use mischief marketing to sell your ideas, too. You can try to convince people that selfishness and greed are the highest values. In fact, selfishness and greed are precisely what Ayn Rand's followers market in those huge, boring books they publish.

But if you do decide to mischievously market the ideals of greed and selfishness the way Ayn Rand did, just be sure you stick to the commandments.

To Readers Who Lean Toward the Left

We are in a new millennium. Capitalism has triumphed over communism, and so the time for moral integrity to enter the marketplace has come at last—not via government intervention, but via the natural market forces themselves. This is not a call to action. It is already happening.

The Internet has opened up vast possibilities for reaching and informing consumers, and for inspiring them, mischievously and otherwise, to take action—all kinds of action, not just buying and selling. The marketplace of commerce is merging with the marketplace of ideas and information.

When shoppers are well enough (and mischievously enough) informed about the difference, say, between a salad dressing made by a family-friendly company that supports charitable causes or provides day care for its employees' children and one made by a company that underpays and abuses its employees, consumers in this new, informed era will do the right thing and will no doubt choose—the cheapest one, the one they always chose.

What did you think I was going to say?

Mischievous Pop Quiz

1. In mischief marketing, contrastive enhancement means:
   a) lowering a prospect's expectations about your offering so you can surprise him or her later with something excellent, which by contrast looks even better.
   b) wearing plaid.

2. These days, everyone is terribly serious about making money. But the main point of mischief marketing is to:
   a) have fun.
   b) have more fun.
   c) make money while having fun.

3. If there's something a little odd about your personality or your offering, you should:
   a) cover it up, like everybody else does.
   b) sit in your house and do nothing until you become perfect and everything in your life becomes perfect.
   c) be honest and forthcoming about it, even if that means having to make fun of yourself.

TACTICAL SUGGESTIONS FOR GETTING YOUR FOOT IN THE DOOR

The title of this chapter pretty much says it all. In fact, in a way, this entire book—all of mischief marketing—really boils down to maneuvering around the so-called old boy network and getting your foot in the door.

The old boy network. Insiders. Confidential sources. Informants. Powerful friends. Connections. Juice. All these are different ways of expressing the fact that, in almost every field, *it's not what you know, it's who you know*. Most of the time, we think of this truth about the world as corrupt or unfair. But is it really?

Doesn't it make sense for people to operate on the principle of "who you know"? Think about it. Would you let just anybody take care of your child? Would you let just anybody mind your house and check your mail while you're away on vacation? Of course not. You'd want someone you know, or someone who is known and trusted by a friend of yours. The same is true of everyone in every field.

Take politics, for example. If you worked in that field, would you want to deal with a person who tapes your personal phone conversations without your being aware of it? Of course not. You want to be careful about being tripped up by such people. You find out something about them before you talk to them. You ask around. You get to know them. It's only natural, and it makes sense.

The question is, how do *you* become one of the people everyone knows, and who knows everyone? How, in other words, do you get your foot in the door? That's where mischief marketing comes in.

Take a look at how one celebrity got a foot in the door and see what we can learn from his experience (pages 140–141). What can we learn from Harrison Ford's story?

Waste Not, Want Not

Nature likes to express herself in many different ways, and she likes to use lots of overlap. Take the human brain, for example.

For many years, scientists thought the brain stored particular memories in particular areas. So your memory of the taste of a slice of cake dipped in a cup of tea, for instance, might be stored somewhere behind your nose, or maybe half an inch beneath your lip.

Thanks to current research, however, we now know that the brain stores information in a host of different ways—that it is less like a filing cabinet and more like a complex web or network of cells and chemicals. In other words, your memory of that slice of cake is actually stored all over your brain, not just in a certain area. (Some of us think it's stored in our hips, too.)

A good mischief marketing campaign often uses multiple ways of reaching the same goal and multiple ways of making *that* goal foster and serve *other* goals. Do you remember how your grandmother used to save the fat from frying bacon so she could reuse it later? It's like that. Well, it's not quite as totally disgusting as that—but you get the general idea. In mischief marketing, nothing goes to waste.

The Surly Carpenter

An actor is having trouble getting a break in Hollywood because he doesn't kowtow the way you're supposed to in the Mecca of Moviedom.

After his film debut—a sixty-second shot at playing a bellhop—a movie executive sits him down and tells him he will never make it in this business. "Your scene wasn't spectacular, my friend. Y'know, when Tony Curtis did a bit part like that in his movie debut, playing a grocery delivery boy, the audience thought, 'There's a movie star!'"

To which the actor replies, "That's funny. I thought they were supposed to think, 'There's a grocery delivery boy.'"

This pattern of brashness with Hollywood VIPs continues for a while, so the actor decides he'd better learn a trade while pursuing his film career. He goes to the library, checks out some books on carpentry, and soon becomes an excellent carpenter.

A producer named Roos takes a liking to the surly man and tries to get an audition for him on a new film. Almost daily, Roos regales the film's director to see the actor, but to no avail, so Roos crafts a ruse. He hires the actor to work as a carpenter near the set of the new film, and he arranges for him to construct a very elaborate door that will take a long time to finish.

One day the break comes. Someone doesn't show up for rehearsal on time, or someone isn't available (this is how these real-life stories really always go, by the

Some scholarly people believe that the world may be a kind of "text" that you can read like a book, or a kind of dream that you can interpret. They might point out that this tale is striking because Harrison Ford was working on an actual door when he got his foot in the door of the film business. In other words, he was both literally and figuratively building a point of entry into the film business for himself.

Now, was Harrison aware of this symbolic connection when it was happening? Did he unconsciously accept a job working on a door at a movie studio because he somehow knew it would "open a door" for him into the movie business?

Or would he just spit at an idea like that if we brought it up to him? Are we ourselves "reading too much" into this story?

In any case, a friend of mine, Mark, once told me about the time he learned how to hunt by studying with a Native American teacher.

They had wounded a deer, but it got away from them, and they had no idea where it had gone. Suddenly, a bird flew overhead. The teacher pointed in the direction in which the bird went and said, "The animal is that way. Let's go."

Puzzled, Mark asked, "Did the bird smell the deer's blood?"

"No," replied the teacher.

"Did the bird see the wounded deer?"

"No."

"Well, then how do you know we should go that way?"

"Because the bird is flying that way."

It took Mark a few minutes to realize that the teacher was following the bird, not because he thought the bird knew anything about the deer, but because he was "reading" the bird's flight path symbolically—in other words, because he was treating the world as though it were a text.

way) and the director needs a replacement—fast—just to read lines for the other actors. And guess who just happens to be available because he is hammering away at a door nearby? Harrison Ford. And the film for which director George Lucas decides that Ford is perfect, based on that fateful reading? *Star Wars*.

Acting as Though

*T*he American philosopher William James was a pioneer of pragmatism—the idea that something can be good not necessarily because you can prove it's true, but because acting *as though* it were true helps you do other things.

In mathematics, for example, if you act as though there really is a square root of –1 (the so-called imaginary number *e*), you can get a lot more math and science accomplished than if you just throw up your hands and say, "I can't believe there is such a stupid, impossible concept!" The difference between high-IQ mathematicians and the rest of us is that mathematicians don't mind working with an idea that is as hard for a human being to grasp as it is for a poodle to understand that, when you're pointing at something, you don't want Fifi to keep following your finger.

So if somebody says to you, "The world is alive with meaning! Look!" don't simply stare at his or her finger and make an easy, sarcastic comment. Instead, let's see what they're pointing at. Let's look at the world.

(And yes, they found the deer in that direction. But I'm not a big fan of hunting, so I'm not going to talk about that part.)

Now, is it really possible to "read" events that happen to you as though they were signs or messages? Probably not. But it is useful to imagine yourself living in such a world.

Do you want to grow a successful business? Do you want to market an important product, service, or idea? Do you want to get across a powerful idea to people? Then start thinking of yourself as a *living* being in a *living* world—not as a cog in a machine, not as a victim of circumstances, not as a dead thing in a dead world.

To believe in a world that has meaning; to believe in a world that interacts with you, that responds to you, that makes sense; to believe in a world that is alive—this act of mental gymastics makes *you* more alive. It makes you alert to new opportunities, more cheerful, more enjoyable to be with, more fun to do business with. It makes you shine, just as Harrison Ford did when he finally got that break. You think more clearly. You assess business situations more astutely and make better decisions. You become more creative. Your offering becomes more fascinating because you become more fascinating, fun, attractive, and engaging.

Discover Your Myth

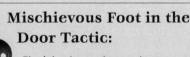

Mischievous Foot in the Door Tactic:

Find (or invent) genuine meaning in the story of your life. It will prepare you to recognize opportunity when it knocks.

In his groundbreaking book *Man's Search for Meaning*, the great Austrian psychiatrist and Holocaust survivor Viktor Frankl says that our primary motivation in life is the search for meaning.

Frankl theorizes that the people who survived the Holocaust were the ones who had a sense of meaning and purpose; they had discovered the myth or story that informed and enriched their lives. Many of the people who died were the ones who lost that sense of meaning.

Think about your favorite character in your favorite movie for a moment. When you feel that your life story is just as important (or as trivial), just as interesting (or as boring), just as big (or small), and just as meaningful as the story of your favorite character in your favorite movie—only then will you discover your myth and harvest the fruit of this mischief marketing technique: the uncanny ability to recognize opportunity when it knocks.

An eccentric but brilliant man gives us an example of what you can accomplish if you see your own story as taking place upon a heroic or mythic stage. He wrote this poem about his belief in past lives:

Through the travail of the ages
Midst the pomp and toil of war
Have I fought and strove and perished
Countless times upon this star.

I have sinned and I have suffered
Played the hero and the knave
Fought for belly, shame or country
And for each have found a grave.

So as through a glass and darkly
The age long strife I see
Where I fought in many guises,
Many names—but always me.

The man who wrote this poem was General George S. Patton, Jr., "Old Blood and Guts," who spearheaded the liberation of France and the defeat of Germany during World War II. His toughness, strict discipline, and self-sacrifice enkindled exceptional pride among his troops. It didn't hurt

Mae Be Mischievous

*I*n mischief marketing, how do you hitch your offering to another's wagon? How do you get others to help carry out your marketing for you?

Well, when your strategy involves mounting a website on a popular subject and then pointing viewers of that site to your own offering, you can use a technique called *parasiting*, which is just a high-tech version of something people have been doing for centuries. (See Chapter 6.)

Mae West showed her mastery of pre-Internet parasiting when, way back in 1926, on the backs of passersby, she mischievously slapped stickers that cited her new stage play, *Sex.* Thus did the hapless strollers become walking billboards for Mae's show.

No chances were taken with the publicity for Sex. *Placards were placed everywhere. "I sent boys all over town with stickers. If you stopped for a minute when one walked by, why you got a sticker stuck clean across your back, with SEX printed on it." The sticker gag would find its way into* Every Day's a Holiday, *where Nifty Baily borrows the same technique.*

—EMILY WORTIS LEIDER
Becoming Mae West
Farrar Straus Giroux,
1997

Patton to think of his life in larger terms, and it didn't hurt us, either, because without people like Patton, we'd all be living in a police state.

Although Mae West had a different sense of her mythos, she, too, defended and marketed many of the liberties we enjoy today.

A life guided by a sense of meaning—however real or illusory that meaning may be—is a life that's not only more fun, but also more electrifyingly open, and alert to opportunities—opportunities that a more "realistic" (and more depressed) person is likely to miss.

If you're having difficulties seeing your life in larger, more mythic terms, practice seeing your life as a movie. The following books might help:

★ *Man's Search for Meaning* by Viktor Frankl, Washington Square Press, 1998.
★ *Rent Two Films and Let's Talk in the Morning* by John W. Hesley & Jan G. Hesley, John Wiley & Sons, 1998. It's about videowork, a therapeutic process in which you watch films that relate to your problems.
★ *The Motion Picture Prescription: Watch This Movie and Call Me in the Morning: 200 Movies to Help You Heal Life's Problems* by Gary Solomon, Aslan Publishing, 1995.
★ *The Mythic Path* by Stanley Krippner, Putnam Publishing Group, 1997.

Sometimes legends make reality, and become more useful than the facts.

—SALMAN RUSHDIE
Midnight's Children
Putnam–USA, 1995

Know Thyself Quiz

★ What kind of myth or story are you living right now?
★ Is your story working for you? Be honest!
★ Is it a sad story about an unrecognized genius? A myth about an inventor who just can't get anyone to believe in her invention? A fairy tale about an entrepreneur who just can't find investors? Or a girl/guy who just can't find the right guy/girl?
★ If you discover you've been living a story like that, get rid of it. Get another story.

Follow Your Unique Hobbies

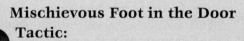

> **Mischievous Foot in the Door Tactic:**
>
> Pursue things you love that you think you don't have time to pursue.

Harrison Ford is now a famous actor, but he didn't become famous by following only his interest in acting. He did it by following his interest in carpentry! Sure, carpentry represented a way of making a living, but he could have made a living in any number of other ways. Even though carpentry had nothing to do with acting, Ford chose it because he liked it. That it happened to be practical, too, was a bonus.

It's just as important, however, to follow the things you like that are not practical, or that don't seem practical at the moment. If you follow the things you love for their own sake, all your offerings in business and in life will take on new color and meaning. You'll find similar advice in a book called *Do What You Love, the Money Will Follow* by Marsha Sinetar, Dell Books, 1989. The title alone speaks volumes.

The story of Galileo (page 146) is not, strictly speaking, a mischief marketing story, but it illustrates the importance of following your unique hobbies as a mischief marketing technique. Why were great scientists like Einstein and Galileo able to see things nobody else could see at the time? Why were they so perceptive?

Harvard professor Gerald Holton and neurologist James Austin say it's not because they were smarter than everybody else, but because such geniuses often pursued highly individual, sometimes eccentric, hobbies

The Shadow Master

The year is 1608, and somewhere in the Netherlands the telescope has just been invented. An Italian guy finds out about the new invention and builds his own homemade model. He uses it to look at the moon, which on its surface displays some puzzling, dark smudges that none of the man's highly intelligent friends can figure out.

Unlike most of his friends, however, the Italian guy once studied art—specifically, a painting technique known as chiaroscuro, a special way of using light and shadow to render three-dimensional objects. This unique background in art enables him to recognize that the dark spots on the moon represent the shadows of mountains.

Once he sees that fact, everyone is suddenly able to see it, and everyone agrees that, yes—ridiculous as it is to even think such a thing in the early 1600s—there are, indeed, mountains on the moon!

That Italian guy's name? Galileo.

and interests that their colleagues didn't give a shilling about. Because they nurtured certain ideas, images, melodies, fascinations, curiosities—in other words certain unique themes—faithfully throughout their lives, people like Galileo and Einstein were prepared to understand things their colleagues just didn't get. These oddball interests laid the foundation for their great discoveries.

Know Thyself Quiz

Make a list of your hobbies and interests. Concentrate on the things you love that nobody else loves. When I say "things you love" I mean ideas you keep thinking fondly about, images that keep running through your mind, or unique interests such as an interest in painted turtles—in other words, things that don't seem to have any practical use to you right now.

Don't Throw Pearls to Swine

Mischievous Foot in the Door Tactic:

Don't bother with people who don't understand what you're doing. Follow your heart and find your own people.

Harrison Ford's story also teaches something else. It illustrates that you can be yourself while you pursue your personal or business goals. You don't have to try to please other people or become what *they* want you to be. Instead of fighting people who don't understand what you're trying to do, go out and find people who appreciate you and your work.

Do not throw your pearls to pigs. If you do, they may trample them under their feet, and then turn and tear you to pieces.

—MATTHEW 7:6

A word of warning: Being yourself does not mean being antisocial or rude. Leave that childish stuff to people who are merely pretending to be themselves. If being yourself means dressing and acting like a Jehovah's Witness or like Bill Gates, by all means do so. Just don't wear a sign that says, "I'm being myself." Don't be insulting or rude to people, unless, of course, that's the real you.

Does my sassiness upset you?
Why are you beset with gloom?
'Cause I walk like I've got oil wells
Pumping in my living room.

—MAYA ANGELOU
"Still I Rise"
1978

Have a Parallel Plan B

Mischievous Foot in the Door Tactic:

Have a parallel backup plan so you can wait comfortably until a door opens for you.

You need to have a backup plan, as Ford did with his carpentry. The balance between Plan A (your long-term dream) and a parallel Plan B (your short-term way of making a living) is a delicate one. It's practically a tightrope walk.

The sign painter's story (on page 148) illustrates that delicate balance.

Did you ever watch a cat wait by a mouse hole or stalk a bird? Most of the time, the cat looks relaxed and comfortable, even bored. But as soon as it spots a chance to pounce, it moves like lightning. That's how you've got

The Sign-Painting Tightrope Walker

One day, a musician with a band realizes that he needs to learn how to walk that age-old tightrope between pursuing a dream and making a living. He decides to try a little mischief marketing.

He uses a simple tactic. When prospects call to ask about his band, he talks fast so he sounds rushed. "See-ya. Okay, gotta go. Bye now." This makes the callers think his band must be very busy and, of course, very good. (See the Wizard of Oz tactic in Chapter 12.) This simple but effective (and mischievous) strategy works so well that the musician eventually starts sending out other bands under his name, on some nights as many as five different bands. He starts making his dream come true. Yet (here comes the balancing act) he is practical enough not only to keep his sign-painting business, but also to tie that business into his music business. How? "When customers came for posters to advertise a dance, I would ask them what they were doing about their music. When they wanted to hire a band, I would ask them who's painting their signs."

That expert tightrope-walking musician's name? Duke Ellington.

Duke Ellington began to realize the significance of the interplay between management and artist and the necessity for it. . . . He had begun to learn the art of hustling in back halls and dark alleys, how to play at top level in places that were prepared for "sport." His mastery of this developed as a parallel until he was no longer a hustler but a businessman.

—JOHN EDWARD HASSE
Beyond Category: The Life and Genius of Duke Ellington
Simon & Schuster, 1993

to be when you're pursuing your goal: comfortable on the one hand, and ready to pounce on the other. Your parallel Plan B makes it possible for you to be comfortable. Your mischief marketing Plan A makes it possible for you to pounce at precisely the right moment.

A mischief marketing parallel Plan B is different from the conservative Plan B idea your relatives may have preached to you. If it were up to your relatives, everyone would have a secure, sensible job at the post office, instead of pursuing "unrealistic" goals and dreams.

Whether your parallel Plan B involves working at the post office, stuffing grocery bags, or writing speeches for politicians, do not allow that backup strategy to replace your true goal. Never say to yourself, "Oh, I'll start working on my true goal as soon as I make enough money licking these floors at the convenience store." Start working on your true goal now. Even if you think you need to continue licking floors for a while to put food on the table, by all means do so, but pursue your true goal at the same time.

In short: Do not put your backup job first. Do not make it your first priority. It's a common mistake.

Don't Procrastinate

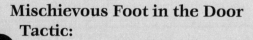

> **Mischievous Foot in the Door Tactic:**
>
> Exorcise the demon Asoonezzeye. Make sure your Plan B is a parallel plan, not a replacement plan.

The Asoonazeye demon can turn you into a procrastinator when it whispers in your ear:

★ "Asoonezzeye make enough money selling cars, I'll start my own business."
★ "Asoonezzeye exercise and lose weight, I'll start dating again."
★ "Asoonezzeye get my degree, I'll look for a job."
★ "Asoonezzeye get an idea like Charlie Darwin's, I'll write something."
★ "Asoonezzeye find a venture capitalist, I'll market my idea."

"You're familiar with the rules concerning exorcism, Damien? Especially important is the warning to avoid conversations with the demon . . . . We may ask what is relevant," said Merrin. "But anything beyond that is dangerous. Extremely. Especially do not listen to anything he says. The demon is a liar. He will lie to confuse us; but he will also mix lies with the truth to attack us. The attack is psychological, Damien. And powerful. Do not listen. Remember that. Do not listen."

—WILLIAM PETER BLATTY
The Exorcist
Harper and Row, 1971

It's easy to mix lies with the truth when thinking about your goals. Yeah, the truth is that you have to earn a living. Yeah, the truth is that you have to be realistic, and face facts squarely. The truth is that you have to sell out and settle down and forget about those stupid dreams you have. Whoa, wait a minute; that last sentence is a lie. See what I mean? Like the demon in *The Exorcist*, the Asoonezzeye demon mixes it all up mightily and merrily: truth and falsehood, good and bad, right and wrong. Do not listen. Do not fall for the "as soon as I . . ." argument.

One other psychological demon that will get in your way as you try to pursue your goals is the nagging inner voice that likes to criticize you. It looks over your shoulder and makes snide comments from time to time about what you're attempting to accomplish. Watch out for this one; it's sneaky.

Learn Something New

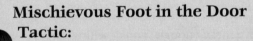

Mischievous Foot in the Door Tactic:

Learn something new while you're waiting for your break.

When you do mischief marketing, you don't have to obsess about your goals. In fact, you shouldn't. To obsess about your projects would be contrary to the spirit of this marketing practice. Instead, learn something new. Harrison Ford learned about carpentry, but you can learn about anything you like.

Learning something new helps you achieve your goals because you usually have to go to new new places and do new things in order to do so. This keeps you busy, rather than depressed. But learning something new does much more than keep you in good spirits. It exposes you to random information and people that you not might otherwise have seen or encountered.

You may have heard of a phenomenon called *synchronicity*. The term was coined by Swiss psychologist Carl Jung, who used it to mean "meaningful coincidence." What is synchronicity? Meg Lundstrom's quote (next page) gives a pretty good idea.

Learning carpentry enabled Harrison Ford to go places and meet people he would not otherwise have met. This included producer Fred Roos, of course. The new skill also brought him into close proximity with movie people, which in turn gave him a chance to find out what roles were being auditioned, who was directing what movie, and so on.

There are things you can do to increase the number of useful coincidences or synchronicities in your life. Among these techniques is learning something new.

 The uncanny coincidence. The unlikely conjunction of events. The startling serendipity. Who hasn't had it happen in their life? You think of someone for the first time in years, and run into them a few hours later. An unusual phrase you'd never heard before jumps out at you three times in the same day. On a back street in a foreign country, you bump into a college roommate. A book falls off the shelf at the bookstore and it's exactly what you need. . . .

Is it only, as skeptics suggest, selective perception and the law of averages playing itself out? Or is it, as Carl Jung believed, a glimpse into the underlying order of the universe? He coined the term synchronicity to describe what he called the "acausal connecting principle" that links mind and matter. He said this underlying connectedness manifests itself through meaningful coincidences that cannot be explained by cause and effect. . . .

Some scientists see a theoretical grounding for synchronicity in quantum physics, fractal geometry, and chaos theory. They are finding that the isolation and separation of objects from each other is more apparent than real; at deeper levels, every-thing—atoms, cells, molecules, plants, animals, people—participates in a sensitive, flowing web of information. Physicists have shown, for example, that if two photons are separated, no matter by how far, a change in one creates a simultaneous change in the other.

—MEG LUNDSTROM
flowpower.com

Related to synchronicity is the small world theory. People sometimes refer to this theory by talking about "six degrees of separation"—an expression used by John Guare in his play of the same name.

As explained in Chapter 6, a degree of separation is a friend or acquaintance who separates you from somebody else. There would be zero degrees of separation between you and your closest friends. According to the theory, there are only six degrees of separation between you and any other person on the planet. In other words, we are all closely related to each other without even knowing it. This sounds a little crazy, but it's actually well supported by mathematical probability theory. Following is a true list of separations between the author of this book and the Pope.

★ Ray (the author of this book) vaguely knows
★ Steve and Elaine Wynn (casino people) who know
★ Bill Gates (the computer guy) who knows
★ Barbara Walters (the TV interviewer who makes everybody cry) who knows
★ Every human being on earth—including the Pope.

Okay, okay. So maybe Walters doesn't know the Pope, but you get the gist, which is that there are only about five or six people between you and the Pope, or between you and Jerry Falwell. This is why you should immediately start thinking about investing in a bomb shelter.

Mischievous Pop Quiz

1. Mischief marketing is about getting around:
   a) old boy networks.
   b) the confederacy of dunces that dominates most industries.
   c) clubs run mostly by little men with little minds.
   d) all of the above.

2. If you can discover your myth:
   a) your life will have more meaning and joy.
   b) you'll project the kind of confidence that makes people successful.
   c) you'll turn into a wacky New Age weirdo.
   d) choices (a) and (b)—and maybe (c), if you get carried away.

3. It's a good idea to study synchronicity because:
   a) it helps you envision the possibility that your life has meaning and purpose.
   b) it introduces new people and new information into your life.
   c) it rhymes with schmynchronicity.
   d) all of the above.

4. William James said that for an idea to be useful and productive:
   a) it has to be true.
   b) it has to be both true and provable.
   c) it doesn't have to be either true or provable.

TACTICAL SUGGESTIONS FOR CREATING CREDIBILITY (OR GETTING AROUND THE DREADED CATCH 22)

Can you believe that, at one time, few people had ever heard of most of the people whose "origin tales" we've documented in this book—people such as Bill Gates, Barbra Streisand, and Ted Turner? Before these celebrities became household names, many of the people who knew them weren't particularly impressed by them. Almost nobody took them seriously.

Why weren't they taken seriously? If they're as brilliant as they seem to us today, shouldn't their abilities have been obvious all along? Why didn't people always hang on their every word, as they do today? Why didn't they always have the throngs of worshipping fans they now have? Why didn't people instantly recognize their abilities? The answer is simple: when these now-famous people were first starting out, they had no track record, no credibility.

In a moment, we'll revisit the story about Steven Spielberg and study that tale step by step in order to see how he solved this particular problem. Later, we'll see how others met the credibility challenge and emerged triumphant.

Since you're still reading this book, it's a safe bet you'd like to find an outlet for your ideas, your work, or just for yourself. You may also hate

> [Walt] Whitman was adept in the art of self-promotion—frequently writing anonymous reviews of his own works, or preparing defenses and explanations that he published over the signatures of obliging friends.
>
> —A. H. SAXON
> *P. T. Barnum: The Legend and the Man*
> Columbia University Press, 1989

153

marketing or selling. Yet you know that, eventually, you'll need to market yourself or your offering. If, however, you currently have little or no credibility—or if your fledgling company doesn't have a proven track record—then you're in the same situation in which every one of these noteworthy people once found themselves.

You could very well be the next Bill Gates, Steven Spielberg, or Mother Teresa, only nobody knows it yet. So what can you do about this?

Think of all the really successful men and women you know. Do you know a single one who didn't learn . . . the trick of calling attention to himself in the right quarters?

—STORM JAMESON
A Cup of Tea for Mr. Thorgill
Harper & Bros., 1957

Well, you've got two choices—the same choices that were once before Gates, Streisand, Turner, Duke Ellington, Benjamin Franklin, Harrison Ford, Estee Lauder, the Bee Gees, and others mentioned in this book and on the mischiefmarketing.com website:

★ Choice 1: to complain about the fact that people don't immediately recognize an offering like yours when they see it.
★ Choice 2: to accept the fact that people don't immediately recognize an offering like yours when they see it.

Choice 2 is the one successful people make. Not that there's anything wrong with choice 1. It's okay to complain now and then. In fact, it's healthy to complain—up to a point. At least one psychologist recommends that, to maintain a healthy psyche, you need to allow yourself about ten minutes per day of unrelenting whining. But in the end, choice 2 is the one that allows you to get on with your task or your mission.

We need two kinds of acquaintances, one to complain to, while to the others we boast.

—LOGAN PEARSALL SMITH
Afterthoughts
Constable, 1931

What you want to move on to is creating credibility so you can help people see the value of your offering. Making an offer is not about you or me (with our fragile pride) but about helping people. It's about sharing your gift with them. It's about giving people something that will be of lasting value to them, whether it's your knowledge, your skill, your product, your novel, your invention, your moral perspective, your screenplay, your textbook, your software program, your recipe collection, your theory about democracy, your sense of humor, or your love of cats.

There is no good in arguing with the inevitable. The only argument available with an east wind is to put on your overcoat.

—JAMES RUSSELL LOWELL
Democracy and Other Addresses
Houghton Mifflin, 1887

Your acceptance of other people's apparent limitations is your first step toward generating the credibility you need to present your offering to the world. If you can purge yourself of the natural tendency to get frustrated with your prospects' apathy, you'll get a green light to enjoy winning (not demanding) their attention. Put your ego aside, and you can transform the marketing of your offering into so much fun that, half the time, you'll be bursting with joy and anticipation about the whole thing. Your biggest problem will be containing your glee so you don't get too happy about opening the presents that spring from your mischievous projects. Remember Shakespeare: *The play's the thing.*

Judge Not

Mischievous Credibility Tactic:
Stop judging people for superficially judging you.

You've been trying every imaginable tactic to showcase your offering. You've been shining like the sun on a beach to bring it to the attention of someone who really understands, but to no avail. At this point, you may conclude that everybody you meet is stupid, blind, selfish, or all of the above. But that's only half true.

> *Americans have a wealth of material resources, but a poverty of time.*
>
> —MOTHER TERESA OF CALCUTTA

The simple truth is that most people are just too freaking busy to understand what you're talking about. They are so busy they don't even know what to pay attention to in their own personal lives. How can you expect them to pay attention to you? After all, they have to *look* at you before they can *see* you. They have to *listen* to you before they can *grasp* what you're about.

Unless you're a saint, you're probably the same way. We're all that way. We're human. (If, on the other hand, you *are* a saint, please forward my apologies to the Vatican.) If you doubt that you perhaps sometimes judge people superficially, take a moment to do two simple "imagination workouts" before you proceed with the rest of this chapter.

"Judge Not" Imagination Workout #1

Imagine that the year is 1970 and that you have never heard of Bill Gates. Think about his glasses, his freckles, how he talks, how he dresses, how he moves. Now ask yourself: if you met him back then, would you vote him most likely to succeed, or most eligible bachelor, or most likely to be the richest human being on earth? Probably not, unless you're psychic. I know that I would not have given you a dime for any one of those propositions back in 1970.

> *The weak can never forgive. Forgiveness is the attribute of the strong.*
>
> —MAHATMA GANDHI

"Judge Not" Imagination Workout #2

Think back on your day today. Whom did *you* ignore or dismiss for one reason or another? Whom did *you* judge or look down on? Was it the clerk at the convenience store? Somebody with purple hair and a pierced body part? Somebody on the phone with an irritating voice? A telemarketer? Your mother? Your son? Al Gore?

What was your basis for ignoring them? Be honest now! Wasn't it something totally superficial, something about the way they talked or moved? Wasn't it something about their clothing, their job, their age? Or were you so busy that you didn't even have time to register the incident at all until just now?

Now imagine that it's five years from now, and one of these people—somebody you ignored today—has become a famous writer, a renowned talk-show host, a great musician, a brilliant business leader, or a genuinely loving religious leader. Will you honestly be able to claim that you spotted the person's talent at the outset? Will you be able to say that the person enjoyed the same credibility with you in the past as he or she will have five years hence? Probably not.

If you performed these two simple exercises honestly, you quickly saw that the people you are trying to reach are usually "ignoring" you for exactly the same reason you ignore others: They don't know you. Or perhaps they know you too well (your family probably falls into this category). Or they know you only as a page on the Senate floor named Billy Clinton, not as the future president of the United States. In other words, there's no signal that tells them, in effect, "Pay attention!" or "Heads up!" or "No more bets, please! We have a winner!"—unless you create such a signal.

So remember: judge not!

With that vital first step behind us, let's discuss the nuts and bolts of creating credibility.

We'll start by taking apart the Spielberg story you saw at the beginning of the book to see what we can learn from it. The full story is reproduced on the next page.

Michael Jackson's Bizarro World Twin

*T*hroughout the history of mischief marketing, women have posed as men (Sophie Germain) and men have posed as women (Ben Franklin) in order to boost their credibility. One white jazz clarinetist boosted his musical credibility by posing as a black man.

> [Milton "Mezz"] Mezzrow was a white Jewish man—his real surname was Mesirow—who successfully fobbed himself off as being black; he even registered in the Army as a white-skinned black (he called himself 'a voluntary Negro'). Although Mezzrow was ridiculed by many of his contemporaries, to the Brooklyn jazz buffs the idea of even approximating being black, of becoming that much closer to the music they loved, was heady stuff.

—ERIC LAX
Woody Allen: A Biography
Knopf, 1991

The Universal Squatter

A prospective filmmaker sneaks onto the lot of Universal Studios and sets himself up in an empty office on the premises. He even buys some plastic letters and mounts his name in the building directory. The security guards greet him every morning. They think he belongs there. (He certainly acts like he does.)

Eventually, his mischief marketing pays off. He gets studio executives to view his first films, and, impressed, they grant him his first directing break. From there, he goes on to become the most successful director in the history of the film industry. The seventeen-year-old prospective filmmaker's name? Steven Spielberg.

> *The quality of mercy is not strained, It droppeth as the gentle rain from heaven upon the place beneath: it is twice blessed; It blesseth him that gives and him that takes.*
>
> —WILLIAM SHAKESPEARE
> *The Merchant of Venice*
> Act IV, Scene 1

> *If you don't stop with these billions of cutesy quotes, I'm going to push you right out the window.*
>
> —AUTHOR'S INNER DEMON

Now, you may read this account and think "Well, *I'm* certainly not going to break into a movie studio and then try to look as though I belong there. This story has nothing to do with me or with my business."

But think again. Is this really just a story about breaking into a movie studio? Is it just a story about setting up a bogus office? Isn't it really a story that shows how to look like you already belong there—wherever "there" is for you?

Do unto Others

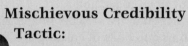

Mischievous Credibility Tactic:

To get acknowledgment, give acknowledgment.

Spielberg's story tells us that Steven was friendly to the security guards at the movie studio. And although it doesn't say so in the story above, he also befriended an on-site librarian who got him a temporary pass to Universal's inner sanctum. (He didn't really break in every day.) In other words, he was hospitable to people who normally don't get recognized very often themselves. In his effort to get acknowledged, he acknowledged others.

So what's the essence here? If you want to be acknowledged for your work or your talents, start acknowledging other people; not only the people around your prospect, but people everywhere. And don't wait until you get famous. Start now.

Let's say you're trying to get an appointment with the CEO of a large company, but it's nearly impossible. Your research discloses that her husband is active in the field of education. You also learn that, because he's usually overshadowed by his more famous spouse, he rarely gets acknowledged for his hard work. What can you do?

Here are some possibilities to jog your mischievous imagination:

★ Write a carefully crafted letter to the spouse about how much you admire his work.
★ If you don't genuinely admire his work, do not do this.
★ If possible, strike up a friendship based upon your letter.
★ Later, at an appropriate time, bring up the subject of how hard it is to see his spouse. Without your even asking, he will probably offer to introduce you to her. He may even help her see the value of your offering. And if not, you'll have made a new and interesting friend. (Remember the knight fork tactic!) In fact, you may even like your new friend better than the CEO.

Keeping in mind that Elton John became a gofer in order to get access to a recording studio, start with a list of people around your prospect who work hard but don't get much attention. Such a list might include: gofers, secretaries, assistants, mailroom personnel, receptionists, younger brothers or sisters (especially in a family-owned business), members of the technical crew (on a TV show, say), and junior writers or editors.

Now ask yourself: How can you acknowledge these people? What can you find out about them? What are they interested in? What are their goals and aspirations? How can you help them fulfill their dreams and get the acknowledgment they deserve?

A word of advice about being sincere. People will see right through dishonesty, and they will conclude (correctly) that you're just kissing up to them to get to the boss. If you don't believe this, try being dishonest

sometime, and see where it gets you. Of course, if you're a politician, you can ignore these remarks.

Smile When You Say That

Mischievous Credibility Tactic:
If you do something gutsy to get recognition, do it with humor.

Spielberg's templative tale also shows us that what Steven did was bold and gutsy. It was also humorous. In other words, Steven didn't break into the movie studio and start a fire. He didn't send pipe bombs in the mail like the Unabomber (who, by the way, admitted to killing those people because he wanted to get his ideas published!). No. Instead, Steven set up an office. He did something constructive. And it was something that didn't hurt anybody or take anything away from anybody else. Even if his plan had failed, Steven would always have had a great story to tell his future prospects and friends. When you start orchestrating your own mischief marketing campaign, do it the way Steven Spielberg did it. Do it in a way that won't hurt or embarrass anyone. And do it with humor.

Get a Clue About Class

Mischievous Credibility Tactic:
Carry out your mischief marketing with style and grace.

Spielberg carried out his project elegantly, gracefully—you might almost say artistically. He didn't have to do it that way. He could have just holed up in an office and waited, but he didn't. Instead, the story reveals (if you know how to read between the lines) that he lavished a lot of care and attention on "his" office.

Be sure to pour a lot of heart into your own mischief marketing campaigns. Don't be sloppy or superficial. Treat all your marketing activities—the totality of your presentation—as a labor of love.

Be Excellent

Mischievous Credibility Tactic:

If you don't make your actual offering excellent, your whole campaign will backfire.

The story doesn't tell us this directly, but we already know one essential thing that's implied by this whole discussion: that Steven's offering—the films he eventually got to showcase for the movie executives—was excellent. This points to the first commandment: *Thou shalt not implement a mischief marketing strategy unless thou canst look upon thy work and say, yea, it is good; verily, I like it.*

There are some extremely powerful techniques in this book. But as with all things powerful, they're also potentially dangerous. If your offering itself isn't very good, techniques like these will work against you rather than for you. If your offering isn't all that good, if you didn't give it 100 percent, if it doesn't really please you, use a more conventional strategy instead, one that's less likely to backfire. Take out a newspaper ad or a radio spot.

The Kahnfidence Man story is also about the challenge of creating credibility. This tale comes in two parts. The first part is here. The second part is in the section on the Vulcan tactic in Chapter 12.

The Kahnfidence Man (Part I)

*A*n immigrant comes to the United States and stages a complex scenario.

He rents a small office (because he doesn't have enough money for a big one). Then, to make his budding company look busy, he enlists his friends to pose as employees.

On a certain day, a representative from an important magazine comes over. Upon his arrival, the immigrant's friends start scurrying around the office. They call each other on their phones and type away madly on their computers.

Impressed with this flurry of activity, the representative jumps at the opportunity to extend the immigrant a $10,000 credit to place a full-page ad. That ad runs in *Byte* magazine, and the program today known as SideKick—the first software product to be sold by mail—becomes a huge success within a few weeks.

That immigrant is Philippe Kahn, and his company is Borland, one of the biggest and best of the early computer companies.

This story teaches an important lesson that applies to the fiercely competitive time in which we live. Today, we need each other more than ever. Now how can we adapt this tale?

Well, much of the time, you probably try to do too much work by yourself. This happens because a lot of us have a misguided, pioneering attitude of, "I'm going to do it all myself. I don't need anybody's help." But that is an antiquated approach from an era long gone. The world has changed, and so must the pioneers.

Call on Friends

Mischievous Credibility Tactic:
Get by with a little help from your friends.

Philippe Kahn didn't try to do everything himself. He asked his friends to pitch in and help him build his credibility, and they gladly did. In fact, they probably had a lot of fun doing it.

Each friend represents a world in us, a world possibly not born until they arrive, and it is only by this meeting that a new world is born.

—ANAIS NIN

Know Thyself Quiz

To find out if you're making the most of your friends and contacts, ask yourself these questions:

★ Do you have friends or acquaintances who will help you market or present your offering in the best possible light?

★ If your answer is no, where can you find them? If your answer is yes, where can you find more of them?

★ What associations can help you meet people who might have fun helping you? Are there any trade or professional organizations

Be sure to pour a lot of heart into your own mischief marketing campaigns. Don't be sloppy or superficial. Treat all your marketing activities—the totality of your presentation—as a labor of love.

Be Excellent

> ### Mischievous Credibility Tactic:
>
> If you don't make your actual offering excellent, your whole campaign will backfire.

The story doesn't tell us this directly, but we already know one essential thing that's implied by this whole discussion: that Steven's offering—the films he eventually got to showcase for the movie executives—was excellent. This points to the first commandment: *Thou shalt not implement a mischief marketing strategy unless thou canst look upon thy work and say, yea, it is good; verily, I like it.*

There are some extremely powerful techniques in this book. But as with all things powerful, they're also potentially dangerous. If your offering itself isn't very good, techniques like these will work against you rather than for you. If your offering isn't all that good, if you didn't give it 100 percent, if it doesn't really please you, use a more conventional strategy instead, one that's less likely to backfire. Take out a newspaper ad or a radio spot.

The Kahnfidence Man story is also about the challenge of creating credibility. This tale comes in two parts. The first part is here. The second part is in the section on the Vulcan tactic in Chapter 12.

The Kahnfidence Man (Part I)

*A*n immigrant comes to the United States and stages a complex scenario.

He rents a small office (because he doesn't have enough money for a big one). Then, to make his budding company look busy, he enlists his friends to pose as employees.

On a certain day, a representative from an important magazine comes over. Upon his arrival, the immigrant's friends start scurrying around the office. They call each other on their phones and type away madly on their computers.

Impressed with this flurry of activity, the representative jumps at the opportunity to extend the immigrant a $10,000 credit to place a full-page ad. That ad runs in *Byte* magazine, and the program today known as SideKick—the first software product to be sold by mail—becomes a huge success within a few weeks.

That immigrant is Philippe Kahn, and his company is Borland, one of the biggest and best of the early computer companies.

This story teaches an important lesson that applies to the fiercely competitive time in which we live. Today, we need each other more than ever. Now how can we adapt this tale?

Well, much of the time, you probably try to do too much work by yourself. This happens because a lot of us have a misguided, pioneering attitude of, "I'm going to do it all myself. I don't need anybody's help." But that is an antiquated approach from an era long gone. The world has changed, and so must the pioneers.

Call on Friends

Mischievous Credibility Tactic:
Get by with a little help from your friends.

Philippe Kahn didn't try to do everything himself. He asked his friends to pitch in and help him build his credibility, and they gladly did. In fact, they probably had a lot of fun doing it.

Each friend represents a world in us, a world possibly not born until they arrive, and it is only by this meeting that a new world is born.

—ANAIS NIN

Know Thyself Quiz

To find out if you're making the most of your friends and contacts, ask yourself these questions:

★ Do you have friends or acquaintances who will help you market or present your offering in the best possible light?
★ If your answer is no, where can you find them? If your answer is yes, where can you find more of them?
★ What associations can help you meet people who might have fun helping you? Are there any trade or professional organizations

When you plan a mischief marketing campaign for your own offering, don't whine about the resources you don't have. Concentrate on what you *do* have and make the most of those. To help you get started, take out a sheet of paper and list at least thirty-five people and things that are your resources. Above all, cultivate an attitude of gratitude.

Thought is a process of exaggeration. The refusal to exaggerate is not infrequently an alibi for the disinclination to think or praise.

—ERIC HOFFER
The Passionate State of Mind
Harper & Row, 1955

Gratitude is not only the greatest of virtues, but the parent of all others.

—CICERO

Mischievous Pop Quiz

1. Before most of the people featured in this book used mischief marketing to get themselves started:
   a) everyone thought they were wonderful.
   b) people just tripped over themselves in order to get a date or a meeting with an unknown geek like Bill Gates, for example.
   c) they were hounded by well-wishers shouting, "You can do it! Go! Go! Go!"
   d) they were lucky if people didn't laugh at them.

2. The best response to being treated superficially by others is to:
   a) think to yourself, smugly, "Well, *I* never judge people superficially."

b) put their names on a private hit list and then, years later, when you've successfully mischief marketed your offering, go back and slap them silly.

c) realize that people in a mammonite society are too busy to pay attention to their own families, let alone to you and your offering.

3. A mammonite, by the way, is:
   a) someone who worships Mammon.
   b) someone who behaves as though they worship Mammon.
   c) both.

MORE MISCHIEF MARKETING TACTICS: VULCAN, OZ, AND MORE

The Vulcan Tactic

You already heard the first part of a templative tale about Philippe Kahn, but there's more to that story. We left out something else he did that day that was very important. Part II (page 168) tells us what else happened.

One of the most critical things to understand about this sequence is that Kahn did not lie to anyone. He merely set up certain conditions that allowed the prospect to draw his own conclusions.

> **Mischief Marketing Tactic:**
>
> The Vulcan—Let people draw their own (positive) conclusions about you.

Wondering why we call this the Vulcan tactic? Remember Mr. Spock from "Star Trek"? He couldn't lie; it violated his moral code as a native of Vulcan. But if the safety of the Enterprise happened to be at stake, he could, shall we say, allow others to draw their own conclusions—conclusions Spock neither affirmed nor denied (although he might have orchestrated them). The same principle applies here.

In your own applications of this mischief marketing tactic, be sure you keep yourself honest. Do not lie about yourself or your offering. Use the Vulcan tactic. Simply arrange for people to conclude whatever they will.

The Kahnfidence Man (Part II)

Before the man from *Byte* arrived, Philippe prepared a fake advertising budget chart that seemed to show what Borland had spent on various magazines. On this chart, he crossed off *Byte* magazine to make it look as though he'd spent all the advertising money on other magazines and didn't have any left to spend on *Byte*.

Philippe pretended to hide the chart, but he actually left it slightly exposed. Later, while the rep sat at Philippe's desk, he took a peek at it. That fateful peek was a key factor in the rep's decision to extend Philippe the $10,000 credit for the ad in *Byte*.

Mischief Marketing by the Vulcan Turn of a Phrase

In one sense, it would be correct to observe that the art of rhetoric represents a set of strategies for using language mischievously. Here's a story that illustrates a remarkably clever use of language.

> . . . I remember Ted Sorensen saying that in the 1960 campaign when Kennedy went to Texas, the candidate told him to come up with some Irish Catholics who had died at the Alamo. Unfortunately, those with Irish names were all Protestants. So Sorensen wrote, "When Jim Brady, Pat Sullivan, and Jack Kelley died at the Alamo, no one asked them whether they were Catholics."

> —JAMES C. HUMES
> *Confessions of a White House Ghostwriter*
> Regnery, 1997

Let Your Audience Draw the Conclusion

This tale is actually a variation on the simple truth tactic. It also illustrates the technique of allowing your prospects to make their own inferences.

To implement this stratagem, you simply arrange your information in a way that favors one inference over another—like a magician who subtly pushes a particular card at you when he says, "Pick a card, any card."

> In 1960 the Democratic candidate for President faced persistent questions about his Roman Catholicism. . . . Never before had the voters of this predominantly Protestant country ever allowed a Catholic to gain the Presidency. It was heatedly argued that . . . John F. Kennedy would be taking his marching orders from the Vatican.

> Kennedy set out to disarm his opponents with his handicap. He went to a well-publicized meeting of a group of Protestant ministers in Houston. . . .

> To underline the David-and-Goliath aspects, Kennedy's people made two decisions. First, the candidate would go to Houston alone. Second . . . [they would] put the "meanest, nastiest-looking" of the Texas preachers right up in the first row. The national television audience would have no trouble choosing whom to root for.

> —CHRISTOPHER MATTHEWS
> *Hardball: How Politics Is Played—*
> *Told by One Who Knows the Game*
> Summit Books, 1988

Idea Joggers

- What can you do that will allow people to naturally conclude favorable things about you or your offering?
- Can you dress better?
- Can you make your offering look more professional?

Another Vulcan tactic is to arrange circumstances or use visual language to make a certain point without actually saying anything at all.

Sometimes, the Vulcan tactic can have the force and effect of a promissory instrument. You declare that something is (or will be) true, and then you make good on your commitment. You *make* it so.

The Vulcan tactic can also take advantage of the natural tendency of people to gossip, or to see what they want to see.

Or this strategy: by implying that people are already doing a certain thing (which they're not), and then prohibiting them from doing it, you plant the suggestion that people should *want* to do it—and so they do. This is a very effective application of the Vulcan tactic.

The Wizard of Oz Tactic

The Wizard of Oz tactic entails making your business or offering look bigger than it really is. We've already seen this tactic deployed in the stories about Steven Spielberg, Philippe Kahn, and many others.

> ## Mischief Marketing Tactic:
> Find ways to make your business or offering look bigger.

Theater managers have been doing this sort of thing for a long time, especially when they mount a comedy. It's well known that audience members tend to laugh more when they're sitting closer together, so the managers will rope off empty seats and pack everyone in toward front and center.

• Can you make it more real for your prospect? Easier to understand? Easier to visualize?

Fake It 'Til You Make It

Diane Terman Felenstein is currently president of Diane Terman Public Relations. Her clients have included Seagram's, Prestige Cosmetics, Salvador Dali, Universal Pictures, and Colgate-Palmolive. Her story shows how you can stretch the truth to fit the events, then immediately turn around and stretch the events to fit the truth.

Diane got her first job working for a record company. She had no training as a publicist, so she had to create her own crash course in public relations. Figuring she might as well shoot for the moon in her quest to promote Audio Fidelity Records, she called *The New York Times* and naively asked for the "records" department. This led her on a receptionist-befuddling series of telephone hops through the payroll, personnel, and accounts payable departments, until she finally landed in the music department—at which point Diane finally confessed to a staff writer that she had no idea what she was doing as a publicist and had only a few days to

(continued)

prove herself on her new job. This so surprised the reporter that he agreed to see her.

Now, as it happened, Hurricane Donna and the indefatigable Diane had arrived in New York simultaneously. Drenched in the rain and buffeted by the winds coursing through Times Square, Diane had no clue what to say about Audio Fidelity Records. Then, out of the blue, a mischievous idea struck her:

I suddenly heard myself telling the reporter our company was going to be recording the sounds of the hurricane. He seemed interested, so I made the story even bigger. I said we were sending engineers to the roof of our building. The reporter promised to cover the event.

I rushed back to my office and demanded a meeting with my boss. When I told him what I'd done, he roared and hit the roof—with engineers. We added the sounds of toilets flushing, hearts beating, phones ringing, and other effects. . . . [W]hen the story appeared in the Times, *we were swamped with calls from record distributors all over the country. Radio stations were actually asking to buy the record for their special effects libraries. Seeing there was a real market, Audio Fidelity quickly produced the record and, eventually, an entire line of sound effects recordings.*

—MARILYN CROCKETT, DIANE TERMAN FELENSTEIN, AND DALE BURG
The Money Club
Simon and Schuster, 1997

Club owners do it, too. That's why, when you go to a comedy club, you end up sitting at teensy tables, trading elbow-in-eyeball jabs with complete strangers. That happens sometimes because the club is packed, but it happens more often because the club has been made to *seem* packed.

Governments and corporations use the Wizard of Oz tactic all the time. It's not something you find only among disadvantaged devotees of mischief marketing. In fact, throughout history, the Wizard of Oz tactic has been (and continues to be) a primary tool of every dictatorship, institution, corporation, or agency that wants to look bigger and more powerful than it really is. The idea is to create a feeling that you can't fight City Hall, and the tactic works superbly well on most of us. That's why many citizens in a democracy don't bother to vote. They've been fooled into thinking their vote could never stand up against the Great Wizard's money and power. This creates a self-reinforcing belief system.

The Oz tactic can also be applied on the Internet.

Perhaps the most common application of the Oz tactic involves changing your name to something that sounds more important or classy. People have been doing this for a long time. Changing your name entails using the Vulcan tactic as well. After all, people usually just assume that your given name is the same as whatever name you go by. When you introduce yourself by your new name, you don't usually add, "But that's not my given name." In other words, by saying nothing and allowing the assumption to ride, you're actually deploying the Vulcan tactic.

For a list of people (and corporations) who've mischief marketed themselves using new names, visit mischiefmarketing.com.

Sin or Synecdoche? Or: It's Not Who You Know, It's Who They Think You Know

*T*he Vulcan tactic takes many forms. People are willing to infer all sorts of things from the smallest external signs. Parts come to represent wholes. Show people an inch and they extrapolate a yard. For a mischief marketer, however, this trait of human nature is fortunate indeed.

In the following snippet of dialogue, one of the most sought-after speechwriters in history is offering some innocent (but mischievous) advice to Amy, a secretary newly transferred to JFK's White House. Amy is upset that she suddenly has to work punishingly long hours, that the White House job delivers none of the glamour she expected, and that she hasn't been on a date in "a month of Sundays."

What clever James Humes tells her is this:

"Amy, you know where the White House pool is?"

"Yes."

"And you know that powder room right next to it?"

"Uh huh."

"Well, at your morning coffee break, go to that Ladies Room. Fill the basin full of water. Dunk your head. Don't dry it, shake it, and go back to your office, and give me a call in a couple of weeks."

Weeks later she called. "My hair's a mess, but I've had dates with a cultural attaché at the French embassy, a colonel in the Pentagon, and a young congressman. They keep asking me about the trade bill, the tax bill, and what the president's thinking. Well, if I see the president, it's on TV."

"Amy," I replied, "you know the president swims every day."

"Yes."

"He swims nude."

"Yes."

"Jackie never goes there, and not all his companions are male."

"Jamie—you've hurt my reputation."

"No, Amy, I've helped it."

> —JAMES C. HUMES
> *Confessions of a White House Ghostwriter*
> Regnery, 1997

*I*t has been a full year since Carroll O'Connor signed books at Tatnuck Bookseller, Marketplace & Restaurant, but owner Larry Abramoff can still give you the bottom line off the top of his head.

"Five hundred and forty books sold in three hours—three a minute," he says. *"It's impossible to do any more."*

What was Mr. Abramoff's secret? After all, with a celebrity like Mr. O'Connor, who played Archie Bunker in the television comedy "All in the Family," a store can see several gawkers for every book that is bought. To reverse the ratio, whenever Mr. Abramoff schedules a celebrity visit, he employs a little reverse psychology, putting up a sign saying, "Maximum Number per Person—5."

> —GREETA O'DONNELL ANAND
> "Scrappy Retailer Succeeds by Not Going by the Book"
> *Wall Street Journal*, March 10, 1999

The Sound of Anything But Silence

One day, Gus Tomelleri and Marc Loe are sitting around in their tiny office above a grocery store. They're offering a product they love. But six months into business the phones are mute, and the few prospects who do call tend to ask embarrassing questions: Who else is buying your software? How many people work for you? How long have you been in business?

"We don't have enough fluff," Marc remarks.

So Gus gussies up a simulated big-business "call center." First, he wires a mike to his computer; then he gets Marc to call from another phone. Gus answers: "Industrial Edge. This is Gus," and starts taking a pretend order. The computer records everything.

Finally, they use sound-processing software to layer in new voices, as Gus and Marc merrily keep on calling each other, taking "orders," and dubbing in voices until they get a nice office buzz going—something that has the sound and feel of a big business.

After their first ad campaign, the test of the mischief marketing strategy begins—the real calls start coming in. Gus answers, transfers each caller to "sales" (Marc), and then fires up the call center, like the Wizard of Oz cranking up the smoke.

Did it work?

Let's put it this way. Gus and Marc no longer need the piped-in background noise. The real phones are still ringing with real customers and orders. And the anticipated annual revenue for their tiny company is up from zero to $120,000.

Shrink the Pond and the Fish Get Bigger

Politicians and political advisors have an arsenal of mischief marketing weapons. Here is an old trick.

The Mondale rearguard then followed with a tactic that Jerry Bruno had made famous advancing Jack Kennedy in 1960. Partitions were used to make the room as small as possible. "We just packed the joint," Beckel said later. "We threw up a partition that made the room a third the size of the ballroom. You couldn't move in the [expletive deleted] place."

The video stage was set up for what may have been the greatest election-night postmortem con job in history. Mondale lost seven contests out of nine. But that was just the arithmetic. At a few minutes past ten, campaign director Robert Beckel walked into what looked like a crowded ballroom to tell the faithful that Mondale had just carried Georgia. To the NBC viewing audience, the event played like a victory statement.

—CHRISTOPHER MATTHEWS
Hardball: How Politics Is Played—Told by One Who Knows the Game
Summit Books, 1988.

Idea Joggers

- What can you do that will make your offering look bigger, more impressive?
- Can you rent a lavishly appointed conference room for a day?
- Can you nominate your business for some fancy award, then announce that "We've been nominated!"—for whatever award it is?
- Can you take advantage of so-called business incubators? (Visit mischief marketing.com for details on these.)

The Anti-Oz Tactic

Sometimes it makes sense to do the *opposite* of the Wizard of Oz tactic. In this case, you make yourself look smaller and more helpless than you really are.

You don't have to look far to find more examples of the anti-Oz tactic. Marilyn Monroe used it to convey an impression of vulnerability and innocence. Avis used it to implement its famous "We Try Harder" campaign. Amazon.com used it to look like an underdog when Barnes & Noble got onto the Internet. Netscape used it when it approached Janet Reno. Walter Taylor used it. (See Chapter 14.)

Artisan Entertainment—which very successfully mischief marketed *The Blair Witch Project*—often uses both tactics. To independent filmmakers, Artisan represents itself as a smaller, more intimate company than it really is. But to giant video chains like Blockbuster, it boasts of being a major player.

Playing up Your Faults

Got a glaring flaw? Don't hide it. Play it up!

In Chapter 14, we'll read about some ex-cons who embezzled millions of dollars. These days, however (now that they're out of jail), they *play up* their faults by advising accountants on how to detect fraud. What they're doing also represents the judo tactic, which is explained in that chapter.

Scared Straight is another illustration of the anti-Oz tactic. The scary-looking prison inmates featured in that film are more successful at marketing moral values to kids than many teachers or parents because they play up their own faults. They stress very graphically what happened to them as a result of having done a lot of bad

That Cyberbishop: Whatta Gaillot!

Not since the printing press has there appeared a greater vehicle for mischief marketing than the Internet.

Jacques Gaillot used to be the Roman Catholic bishop of the diocese of Evreux, in Normandy. For many years, Bishop Gaillot spoke his conscience on such Church-chafing issues as homosexuality, the ordination of women, and celibacy for priests.

By January 1995, the Vatican had had enough from Gaillot. Calling him to Rome, Cardinal Gantin . . . informed the wayward cleric that in twenty-four hours he would no longer be the bishop of Evreux. Instead, he was to shepherd the faithful in the diocese of Partenia. But where was Partenia?

Partenia is what is referred to in Church parlance as a titular see. It is in fact nowhere, or as close to nowhere as possible. . . . There, the Vatican must have reasoned, Gaillot could preach as much as he liked to a congregation of one: himself.

. . . Gaillot gets in touch with his friend Leo Scheer, media philosopher, author of the book Virtual Democracy. . . .

(continued)

Going Dutch

*B*eing mischievous doesn't always entail being a near-saint like Mother Teresa, a Renaissance man like Ben Franklin, or a publishing genius like Bennett Cerf. Even crooks sometimes mischief market themselves.

Gangsters, now that they had wealth and power, became celebrities, people you hoped to catch a glimpse of, read about, or see represented on the stage. Some high-rolling mobsters, instead of cowering in obscurity, actually sought the visibility and notoriety tabloid coverage could guarantee. Bootlegger Dutch Schultz, born Arthur Flegenheimer, changed his name because "it was short enough to fit in the headlines. If I'd kept the name of Flegenheimer, nobody would have heard of me."

—EMILY WORTIS LEIDER
Becoming Mae West
Farrar Straus Giroux, 1997

things. Playing up your faults is really a kind of credibility-enhancing tactic. That is, people tend to put more stock in what you say if they know you've actually lived through whatever it is you're talking about.

Many twelve-step programs also employ this tactic. Millions of people all over the world benefit from twelve-step meetings every day, so there can't be much doubt about the enormous power of this technique.

Considering that the anti-Oz tactic has something in common with the credibility tactic and with the judo tactic, you can begin to see how hard it is to separate these mischief marketing techniques from one another. They all work together. Like synonyms with slightly different nuances, they have many things in common, and yet they're all a bit different.

Doing the Opposite of What's Expected

You could say that most mischief marketing techniques involve at least some element of doing the opposite of what people expect.

Telling the Simple Truth

We mentioned the simple truth tactic briefly in our discussion of the mischief marketing commandments, but it deserves a fuller treatment.

Silly as it may sound, the greatest of all mischief marketing tactics involves telling the simple truth. No one knows why the truth is so powerful, but it's got to be at least partly because it's unexpected. Who expects you to tell the simple truth? Nobody. That's why it's so shocking and arresting to people when you do. In fact, telling the simple truth is actually a type of marketing shock tactic.

Any expression of simplicity or truth can be shocking.

The great baseball player Joe DiMaggio was almost a living symbol of simplicity. A no-frills, unassuming sports hero, DiMaggio never appeared on cheap TV game shows. He pitched products only once or twice. He gave interviews rarely. He never wrote a book or hosted a talk show. He was a simple guy. You almost never heard about him when he wasn't playing.

Old-time baseball fans say that because they never saw DiMaggio talking to cartoon characters selling cheap phone services or hawking cereal, when the moment finally came for him to step out onto the playing field, it was a memorable event just to watch him stroll across the grass. At that moment, they knew that something special, something unique, was happening. The great Joe DiMaggio was here.

The power of the simple truth is like that. It's like poetry. It makes you wonder about things. It shocks you into awareness.

How can you apply the simple truth tactic to your own mischief marketing? Consider the story of Keith Harrell (page 178).

Presentation/ Orchestration Tactics

> ## Mischievous Presentation Tactic:
> Don't always try to look cool.

As we grow up and learn about the world, we're taught a lot of things that we later find out

Poor Boy Andy

You could write a whole book about the many ways in which Andy Warhol mischievously exposed the art industry as a commercial enterprise. You could write another book about his extraordinary transformation of that message, and another about how he used mystery and ambiguity to cloak his mission. Here's one example of how the young Warhol customized his image to fit whatever picture of him his prospects expected to see.

[Eventually, Andy Warhol] was making enough money . . . to afford a Brooks Brothers suit and trenchcoat, which he wore to go out in the evenings, while assiduously maintaining his poor-boy image for art directors.

—VICTOR BOCKRIS
The Life and Death of Andy Warhol
Bantam Books, 1989

Idea Joggers

- What can you do that will make your business look smaller, more vulnerable?
- Can you get a big company to attack your business unfairly, then go to the press with your David and Goliath story?
- How can you parlay being the underdog into creating the impression that you're therefore more motivated and caring than the big dogs?

A Canny Hitchhiker

*T*he following story about Hunter Thompson (author of *Fear and Loathing in Las Vegas*) shows how effective it can be to reverse the Wizard of Oz effect and make yourself look smaller or more helpless than you really are:

Their first rule of the road was to pick up every hitchhiker. In western Kansas, Semonin stopped for a man carrying a five-gallon gas can. When the hitchhiker got into the backseat, he flipped the latches on the can to reveal that it was stuffed with clothes. "No one will pick you up if they think you're a hitchhiker," he explained. "You have to be a motorist in distress."

—PAUL PERRY
Fear and Loathing: The Strange and Terrible Saga of Hunter S. Thompson
Thunder's Mouth Press, 1992

10-10-MISCHIEF Saves Money on Your Long-Distance Phone Bills

*D*id you know that behind many of those supposedly smaller and cheaper 10-10 long-distance phone companies there lies . . . the giant AT&T? One company executive explained the rationale behind a huge company posing as a small one (reversing the usual Wizard of Oz tactic). Note his comment about humor. With this tactic, a serious brand can act like a sillier, more mischievous one.

Howard McNally, president of AT&T Transition Services, which oversees AT&T's dialaround business, says AT&T decided to offer the service under a different name when it entered the market last year because "some people don't want to buy a brand, they think [10-10] is a better bargain." In addition, he adds, "It allows us to be different . . . a little cute, very humorous, which isn't in AT&T's brand image."

—KATHY CHEN
"Some Consumers Attack Long-Distance Ad Claims"
Wall Street Journal, November 4, 1999

Mischief Marketing in Film—Roxanne

*I*n the 1987 film *Roxanne*—loosely based on Edmond Rostand's *Cyrano de Bergerac*, a play that has captured the imagination of readers for over 100 years, and inspired a raft of adaptations—Steve Martin plays C. D. Bates, a man with a big nose and an even bigger crush on a beautiful blond (Daryl Hannah).

Too shy about his physical handicap to declare his love openly, Bates decides to assume the role of a coach for the handsome Chris (played by Ross Rossovich), writing love letters to Roxanne in Chris's name and offering general romantic counsel.

In the happy ending, when Roxanne finally discovers that the touching letters are really from Bates, she accepts and loves him for who he really is.

There is one particularly hilarious scene in the film in which a jerk in a bar tries to insult Bates. Bates counterattacks with a string of insults, all of them funnier than the original. This scene illustrates the mischief marketing tactic of making your shortcomings explicit whenever they are so obvious that your prospect can't ignore them.

are not true. And the things we're told about marketing and selling are no exception.

For instance, most of us have been told over and over again to put our best foot forward because we'll never have a second chance to make a good first impression. But this advice is not always correct.

Think about it: If there were easy, surefire rules for success, everybody would be using them. And everybody would be just as successful at marketing a business or at making art, literature, or music as we are at the easy, surefire task of sitting on a couch chomping tortilla chips and watching "Seinfeld" reruns.

To learn something genuinely new about meeting the challenge of presenting yourself or your offering, let's think about the Streisand story again.

The first thing to notice about this tale is that from the moment she stepped into the audition situation Streisand did not do what everybody else there was doing—trying to look cool. In fact, she went out of her way to look *un*cool. This had the effect of making her stand out from the crowd even before she did anything on stage.

Of course, this kind of strategy is risky. After all, if you stand out from the crowd because you're a little weird, you'll want to correct that impression as soon as possible. In other words, this is a two-pronged strategy.

A Side of Maggots with Your Filet Mignon?

Mother Teresa often did the opposite of what people expected. The result was usually a powerful lesson, mischievously marketed.

In 1992, for example, she flew to New York to be presented with a $100,000 award by the Knights of Columbus. At a white-tie banquet attended by 1,000 members of America's Catholic elite, Mother Teresa was accorded the kind of roaring adulation usually reserved for rock stars or the pope. Before the feast began, the diminutive nun chastened the throng by describing how it took her three hours to pick maggots from the body of an emaciated Calcutta derelict. Then, as was her custom, she left before eating because she felt it inappropriate to dine ostentatiously. An additional $100,000—equal to the cost of the banquet—was later presented to her.

—MICHAEL SATCHELL
"Death Comes to a Living Saint"
U.S. News & World Report, September 15, 1997

Show me a guy who's afraid to look bad, and I'll show you a guy you can beat every time.

—RENE AUBERJONOIS

Touch Them with the Truth

Professional motivational speaker Keith Harrell now collects a fee of about $10,000 every time he speaks. But it wasn't always that way.

In fact, when he first got started, agencies wouldn't even talk to him. So Keith set up his own business in his bedroom, hired someone to answer his phones, and delivered speeches to schools. He did okay, but not great.

One day, he hired an editorial consultant to pull apart his speech, "Attitude is Everything." That's when things really got interesting. Editorial consultant Danella Fogle was mischievous enough to take one of Keith's most heartwarming hard-luck anecdotes (a true and simple story) and move it to the front of his presentation.

Now Keith steps out before his audiences and unexpectedly launches into that true, simple, up-front story—the account of how, when asked to introduce himself on his first day in kindergarten, he stuttered, of how embarrassed he was when the kids teased him, of how he cried and ran home to mom, and of how:

> *My mom just squeezed me. I'll never forget her words. She said, "Honey, mommy just hung up from Miss Peterson. Mommy was coming to get you. Mommy's got some good news. I'm proud of you because you tried. . . . One day my little man is going to stand tall. One day you're going to say your name as loud and as well as the other boys and girls." . . . I'm going to finish something my mother told me I'd be able to do: My name is Keith Douglas Harrell.*

—ELLEN JOAN POLLOCK
"Successful Motivational Speaker Believes 'Attitude Is Everything'"
Wall Street Journal Interactive,
March 2, 1999

Mischief Marketing in Film—*Mr. Smith Goes to Washington*

Let's turn to the movies again for an example of the simple truth tactic. America is one of the few countries to define itself not so much in terms of what its citizens own, what they look like, or who their ancestors were, but in terms of *ideals*—specifically, ideals about democracy and freedom of expression.

Many of Hollywood's finest directors have mischievously used movies as a vehicle for marketing such visions of America, and Frank Capra was better at marketing ideals than almost anyone else.

In *Mr. Smith Goes to Washington*, Capra tells the story of an innocent patriot (Jeff Smith, played by Jimmy Stewart) who gets railroaded into politics by corrupt power brokers who try to turn him into a rubber stamp for their crooked financial scams.

When Jeff wakes up to what's really going on and starts telling the truth about it to the public, one of the senators tries to make Jeff's honesty look like *dis*honesty by calling Smith's statements a "shameless performance for the newspapers—a versatile performance, I grant you, but one that brings his rank down to the level of a sideshow entertainer." (You might call this smear marketing.)

The film culminates in a moving scene in which Smith stages a filibuster. During his long, courageous speech, he uses the power of the simple truth to expose the shenanigans he has discovered. As you can well imagine, telling the simple truth in the context of the Senate is a strange, impertinent, if not downright stupid thing to do, but Smith applies the tactic so masterfully that one of the crooked

Mischievous Presentation Tactic:

Use a surprise attack.

The next thing we learn from Streisand's story has to do with the element of surprise. Everybody loves a surprise. One way to surprise people is by doing the opposite of what they expect. Another is to set up a low expectation and then deliver a high-quality offering.

In this tale, Streisand first set up a low expectation in the minds of her auditioners. Because she was so uncool, they concluded that she didn't have much talent. When they finally heard her sing, they were very surprised. Apple founder Steve Jobs (Chapter 1) did a similar thing when he showed up at important meetings dressed like a slob. The contrast between his presentation and his offering enhanced the perceived value of the offering.

Some years ago, comedian Andy Kaufman used a similar mischief marketing tactic. Kaufman eventually became a star of the hit TV series "Taxi," but at the beginning of his career, when he was unknown, he had a very unusual act.

He'd come on stage looking extremely shy and nervous. Speaking in a peculiar accent (which later became the character Latke's accent), he told some bad jokes. Then he did some even worse impressions. The whole skit was painful to watch. If you were in the audience or viewing it on TV, you laughed only because you didn't know what else to do.

Then Kaufman would announce that he was going to do his impression of Elvis Presley. You laughed again, expecting it to be as bad as everything else he'd done so far. At that point, he

senators, who can't stand his pangs of conscience any more, leaps up and confesses his misdeeds to the entire assembly. The film ends with a rousing affirmation of the ideals of true democracy. When this movie was first released, Washington insiders didn't like it at all. Isn't that surprising?

In our own time, democracy will be destroyed not by corrupt senators—or not only by such people—but by political correctness laws that will make it hard to say anything critical without being sued because your free speech offended or threatened someone or because you used a company's trademark when you reported that its products injure or kill people. But Mr. Smith Goes to Washington is a nice movie anyway.

The Gumless Girl

An aspiring singer shows up at a Broadway audition. Shy and clumsy, she can't seem to do anything right. She chatters nervously, and her shoes don't even match. To make matters worse, she's chewing gum. When the moment comes for her to perform, she crudely spits out her gum and sticks it under the seat of a chair. Then she sings.

Her raw talent and the sheer power of her voice mesmerize everyone in the theater. After she leaves, the auditioner decides to follow a hunch and inspect the chair. No trace of gum.

That "shy" singer's name? Barbra Streisand.

would turn away from the camera, adjust the collar on his costume, and start shaking his leg.

When he finally turned around, you (and everybody else in the audience) were stunned. You suddenly saw before you a man with an astonishing physical and behavioral resemblance to Elvis Presley. Kaufman's impression was flawless, riveting, and filled with vitality. No mere mockery of Elvis, it was a powerful, heartfelt homage to The King. The effect was electrifying.

In the field of business presentation theory, this principle is well known. Experts teach us never to put the best material first when we meet with a client or prospect to market a product or idea. Instead, they say:

★ Put the good (but not the best) material first.
★ Follow it with most—but not all—of the best stuff.
★ Move on to some more good material.
★ Close with the remainder of the best material.
★ Top the presentation off with the best stuff.

This orchestrated approach can make the difference between a fine presentation and a deeply powerful one.

Questions to Ask Yourself

★ In what ways can you deliberately lower the expectations of your prospects before you surprise them?
★ What's the weakest part of your offering or presentation? What's the strongest? What's in between?
★ When do you suppose you might not want to present your best material? Are

there circumstances under which you might ask for a commitment from your prospect before you give away the store?

The ploy in Mrs. Doubtfire illustrates the application of at least two mischief marketing tactics:

★ Adopting an alter ego in a case where your own identity may lack credibility.
★ Setting up a sharp contrast in your presentation that makes your offering look all the more attractive for being better than what your prospect has seen or has been conditioned by experience—or maybe by you—to expect.

> **Mischievous Presentation Tactic:**
>
> Give your audience permission to laugh.

In mischief marketing, you usually end up kidding around a lot. Unfortunately, people don't always get the joke—at first. You sometimes need to let them know in advance that it's okay to laugh. In some cases, this telegraphing of "permission" can make or break your presentation, so be sure to pack it into your bag of tricks.

Mischief Marketing in Film—Mrs. Doubtfire

*I*n the 1993 film *Mrs. Doubtfire*, Robin Williams plays Daniel, a divorced father who wants to see more of his children. The court grants him visitation rights, but once a week isn't enough for Daniel. So he resorts to a mischievous ruse. He pretends to be an old Scottish nanny and housekeeper named Mrs. Doubtfire.

Daniel's ex-wife, Miranda, places an ad in the paper calling for a nanny, but Daniel intercepts her ad and alters it so that any respondents will wind up calling a wrong number. Then he himself places a series of calls to Miranda, using different voices and playing different characters who are supposedly applying for the nanny job. (Daniel, by the way, is an actor who specializes in dubbing cartoon character voices.)

Each character he presents to Miranda is worse than the previous one, and it is hilariously obvious after a few calls that none of them is suited to act as a nanny for her children. Miranda starts worrying about finding a good appli-

(continued)

cant. Finally, when Daniel calls as the supposedly qualified Mrs. Doubtfire, the contrast Miranda perceives between this latest applicant and all the previous losers is so stark that she fairly leaps at the chance to hire the old Scottish lady.

Mischievous Pop Quiz

1. The Vulcan tactic:
   a) entails telling the truth, the whole truth, and nothing but the truth.
   b) entails telling the truth.

2. Implementing the Wizard of Oz tactic:
   a) entails making your offering look bigger or more important than it really is.
   b) has something to do with synchronicity.
   c) Either (a) or (b). I can't remember.

3. The anti-Oz tactic:
   a) entails making your offering look smaller or more modest than it really is.
   b) is itself a rather modest name.
   c) choice (d).

The Early History of Laugh Tracks

*I*f you've ever done a production of a play by Edward Albee out in the sticks, you know that the audience is afraid to laugh at some of the most hilarious lines. That's because they think serious theater is supposed to be boring.

The following tale illustrates how an old (but still reliable) vaudeville trick can loosen them up.

As the months went by, Will [Rogers] continued his education in the ways of showmanship. While his jokes usually got a good response, his understated manner was such that sometimes the audience didn't realize he was being funny. So when he was in New York, he arranged for an employee of Jim Minnick's named Fred Tejan to sit in the audience and laugh loudly at the appropriate times.

—BEN YAGODA
Will Rogers: A Biography
Knopf, 1993

ADVANCED
TECHNIQUES

Mirroring Your Prospect

Earlier in the execution of your mischief marketing plan you profiled your prospects by researching their hobbies and interests. In this section, you'll see why you needed to do that investigative work.

If knowing about birth order and astrology can empower you to figure out how to approach your prospect, then knowing how to mirror your prospect can be even more empowering. Matthew Simon's story on page 184 will bring this technique into focus.

Simon never explicitly said, "You see, this computer stuff is just like gardening." He could have said that, but the impact of mirroring is usually more powerful when your prospect is not made glaringly aware of the communication technique you're employing to get across your ideas.

Linguistic mirroring means finding out what topic your prospect is interested in and then subtly using language that relates to that topic. This technique is especially effective when you use it to craft a letter, a business presentation, a customized brochure, a resume, a speech or sermon, a love letter, a report to a corporate executive, a legal brief, or any communication.

Questions to Ask Yourself

★ In what field is your prospect an expert? Better yet, what subject is your prospect genuinely, deeply passionate about? It doesn't have to relate to the job. It could be a hobby or a sport. It might be something you wouldn't expect, like military aircraft, poetry, the history of the buffalo, astronomy, business books, mesmerism, or parenting. It could be anything.

The Ericksonian Computer Guy

Matthew Simon is a trainer based in Massachusetts who specializes in teaching beginners in the computer business.

Matthew recently met a trainee named Pete. After a short interview, Matthew learned that Pete ran a full-service gardening business of which he was quite proud.

"Most people hire one guy for this task, another guy for that, and so on," Pete said in describing his business. "They end up paying ten bills at the end of the month. But when you call me in, I do it all. I cut the lawn, treat it, seed it. I do the bushes, hedges, flowers, and plants. With my service, you get just one bill at the end of the month. Isn't that a better way?"

As soon as Matthew learned this, he understood how to teach Pete computers. For the rest of the session, he mirrored Pete by using a vocabulary that would create a bridge between computers and gardening. He said things like: "Pete, these little utilities work together almost organically." or "As you are learning these things, Pete, you'll gather that it's like planting seeds. You won't be able to see any results for a while, and you might even get frustrated. It will seem like

★ Does your prospect support some cause like education or health care? Does he or she feel strongly about some legislation or social program?

★ What style of writing or speaking do people use in connection with this cause or subject? I don't mean the style your prospect uses; I mean the style people use in talking or writing about whatever subject your prospect is passionate about. For instance, do people tend to use bulleted text when they discuss this subject? Do they talk like preachers? Like football players? Are they literary types who like to use long and syntactically complex sentence structures? What specific words, expressions, or metaphors are specific to this field of interest? Learn them.

★ What interests (or faults) do you share with your prospect? This is an important question because you may not have the time or the inclination to do a lot of research on, say, the evolution of Mayan pictographs. Or you may not want to spend time duplicating their communication style. If you can find an interest you both share, so much the better. Remember, mischief marketing is like wooing.

★ What are your prospect's favorite words or expressions (whether related or not to a particular field of interest)? List them. Later, weave them into your communications with the prospect.

The key point to take from this discussion is that everyone is passionate about something—and it's almost always something for which they aren't famous, or which has nothing to do with their profession. As a mischief marketer, your job is to discover what that something is. You can do that through research, conversations with the prospect, interviews with the prospect's friends or employees (but don't call them interviews), and so on.

At first, you might want to practice this mirroring technique on someone less intimidating than your prospect. Try it out on your spouse, your kids, or your mom. Take note of the results. Do you observe that people listen better when you reflect their own verbal structures back to them? I'll bet you do. I'll bet you'll even be amazed at the difference.

Of course, you need to be careful to do this sort of thing subtly. Don't be absurdly blatant about it. So like, if you're talking? Like to a teenager? Don't like, be, like, y'know, too, y'know, like, obvious. Okay?

General Linguistic Mirroring

People tend to prefer specific words and expressions, but they also tend to favor certain *types* of words. For instance, your husband might favor visual words. In that case, when indicating agreement he might say, "I see what you mean." Your wife, on the other hand, might prefer kinesthetic words ("I have a good feeling about this"), while your best friend might prefer auditory expressions ("Yeah, I hear ya loud and clear.").

Psychologists sometimes explain this phenomenon by saying that people use different "representational systems." What they mean is that visual people process their experiences primarily visually, auditory people process them aurally, and so on. But this is theoretical stuff. It's hard to figure out what people are actually doing inside their heads. We'll leave such speculations to the psychologists.

The same goes for speculations about why or how some of these other tools work. Who cares?

nothing's happening. But gradually, your knowledge will grow, and one day you'll see that your labor has blossomed into a full understanding of computers."

Matthew also explained what an operating system is by mirroring some of the words and expressions Pete had used to describe his business. He said: "The operating system— Windows, for example—is like a full-service program. With a good operating system, the people who create other programs don't have to teach each one of them how to print to the printer or how to paint colors, shapes, or letters on the screen. Each program calls on the operating system to do those tasks. The operating system does it all."

Embedding Metaphorical Expressions

John Atwood once planned a mischief marketing campaign around a well-known prospect we will call Frank.

John's diligent research in the library unearthed a number of newspaper and magazine interviews in which Frank mentioned his love of baseball. So when it came time for John to craft a letter to his prospect, he carefully embedded into his text expressions like these:

- "If I can get an appointment with you, if I can just get to first base, I know I can show you the full scope of this product's features."
- "With your help, we can hit this out of the park."
- "Other, similar products are worthy competitors, but they all strike out on several key features."

John got the account. Embedding metaphors can be a tricky business, however. Here for instance are some things you would *not* want to say in a case like this:

- "So, in conclusion, take a good swing at my product."
- "This product is ready to ship; my company's at the bottom of the ninth."
- "If you build it, they will buy."

Take astrology for example. If you explore it for yourself instead of parroting what the skeptics say, you'll see that it often works. Not always, of course, but often. More to the point, it appears to work better with some people than with others. So guess what? You can use astrology (or any other tool, for that matter) where it works, and throw it out where it doesn't. But in any case, please don't worry about "how" it works. In a business context, that's a waste of time. Leave that sort of question to the scientists.

The best way to think about this linguistic stuff is to realize that we all share a common language and common dialects, but each of us also has an *idiolect*, an unshared communication pattern that's nearly as unique as a fingerprint.

Do you remember how the FBI finally identified Ted Kaczynski as the Unabomber after about sixteen years of investigative failure? (1) They printed his manifesto in *The New York Times*; (2) his brother, David, spotted the piece (a difficult task, considering it was only about 687 pages long); (3) David recognized certain speech patterns as belonging to Ted; and (4) he tipped off the FBI.

During the trial, the prosecution carefully matched up for the jury certain specific words and expressions that had appeared in both the manifesto and in Kaczynski's personal correspondence. Taken together with the physical evidence, this linguistic information won them a conviction. In other words, where all the FBI's fancy, high-tech tools had failed, what finally identified and stopped the Unabomber was linguistics. Does that tell you something about the importance of using these kinds of tools in your mischief marketing work?

Mirroring Speech Patterns

Shira's Linguistic Mirror

If you're lucky enough to meet your prospect face to face, you can also practice mirroring other aspects of his or her speech and behavior, not just vocabulary. For instance, if you're normally a fast talking New Yorker but your prospect is "Prairie Home Companion" star Garrison Keillor, you might want to slow down a bit and stop shrieking at him.

People speak differently according to where they were born and raised. People living in the southern United States, for example, tend to speak more slowly. They actually mistrust people who talk fast. In the South and elsewhere, the expression "fast talkin'" implies "con artist."

People in the northeastern United States, on the other hand, speak more rapidly and tend to be more direct in their approach, even blunt. They sometimes view southerners as disgustingly nice, which makes northerners think that southerners are con artists.

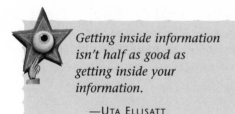

Getting inside information isn't half as good as getting inside your information.

—UTA ELLISATT

Here's an example of how to apply this generalization: Suppose you're fresh from Louisiana, visiting New York City, and you need directions to the Empire State Building. If you walk up to a New Yorker on the street and say, "Excuse me, please, but I was just wondering if you could tell me . . ." you'll get cut off. The New Yorker will

Shira consistently got good grades in college. She even managed to get along with the most ornery professors on campus. No one could figure out how she did it. But Shira had a secret.

While other students were scribbling notes about the subject being taught, Shira was scribbling notes about the linguistic expressions her professors favored. For instance, she noted that one instructor habitually employed words and phrases such as "bizarre," "Western rationalism," "consensus reality," "quick and dirty," "open to the charge of [whatever]," and so on. When it came time to write her papers, Shira would mirror back some of these expressions:

. . . it is not in fact the case, however, that a "quick and dirty" summary of the perhaps bizarre attack on Western rationalism mounted by those postmodern critics for whom a sort of socially constructed or consensus reality is paramount would unavoidably be open to the charge of . . .

It worked every time. Well, almost.

instantly take your excessive courtesy to mean you're up to something suspicious and will probably walk away.

But if you're a mischief marketer, you won't fall into this trap. Instead, you will holler—preferably from across the street—"Hey! Yo! Where the hell is the Empire State Building?" And watch: you'll get a complete and courteously delivered set of directions. In New York, bluntness makes you trustworthy.

Sociolinguist Deborah Tannen has written about this subject at length. In the course of profiling your prospect, you might want to pick up one of her books. You'll also want to read Suzette Haden-Elgin, who writes on different but related linguistic topics. See mischiefmarketing.com for details on all this.

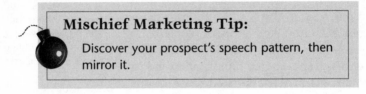

Mischief Marketing Tip:

Discover your prospect's speech pattern, then mirror it.

Advanced Communication Techniques

Mirroring your prospect's language and behavior is easy. It's a comfortable way to develop rapport. But there are other, more difficult communication techniques that are worth mastering.

Embedded Suggestions

One of these techniques has to do with issuing an embedded suggestion. An *embedded suggestion* is a statement to your prospect that you normally would not dare to make without qualification. For instance, it could be a statement like, "You will think this is the greatest thing in the world." Now, if you said something like this directly, you would sound like an idiot. Instead, you embed it within a larger, more acceptable statement, and then you *shift your tone of voice* (subtly!) when you get to the statement you really want to make, the embedded suggestion.

Think back to the example earlier in this chapter about Matthew, the trainer, and his student Peter. During their first computer lesson, Matthew used an embedded suggestion. He told Pete, "As you're sitting there watching the screen, and as you're wondering what I'm doing, and whether *you will understand all this one day*, I am also sitting here and I am hoping *one day you will think this is the easiest thing in the world.*"

You can distinguish the suggestion from the surrounding language by lowering or raising your vocal volume slightly, by slowing down, by using a slightly different accent, or by otherwise marking the communication in a subtle way.

You need to set up certain preliminary conditions (make certain statements) before you use an embedded suggestion. Note, for instance, that Matt made a number of undeniably true statements before he got to the suggestion—statements like ". . . you're sitting there watching the screen . . . ." He also openly acknowledged what Pete was probably thinking with this phrase: ". . . you're wondering what I'm doing . . . ."

Preliminary statements that are undeniably true prepare the prospect to receive the suggestion that follows. This is sometimes called *creating a yes set*. You keep the prospect on the track of thinking, "Yes, that's true. Yes, that's true, too. Yes. Yes . . ." until you finally get to the statement that under less favorable circumstances the person might have resisted (*"you will understand all this one day"*) but to which he or she is now more likely to say yes.

By the way, most of these techniques are covered in various books about the genius Dr. Milton H. Erickson of Phoenix, Arizona. Milton Erickson was an incredible physician and the founder of what is today known as brief psychotherapy. Erickson liberated many people from the terrible psychological and sometimes physical illnesses that made their lives miserable before they met the good doctor. His work forms much of the basis for neurolinguistic programming, for "naturalistic" hypnosis, and for many other spin-offs.

Erickson didn't always take credit for his accomplishments. In fact, he was so subtle in his work that many of his patients had no idea he had cured them. Their problems would disappear, but they didn't always know how or why. They often didn't make the connection to having visited Erickson. They simply thought that they had visited a nutty doctor in Arizona and then, by some coincidence, got cured. But Erickson wasn't interested in getting credit from his patients; he was just interested in seeing them cured. He did get accolades from his colleagues, however, who came from all parts of the country to observe his work.

If you want to read an inspirational book about Erickson, pick up *Uncommon Therapy* by Jay Haley. Even if you subscribe to *The Skeptical Inquirer* (I do), I promise that you will find *Uncommon Therapy* to be a work of literature, if not of science. You will also find that such literature can inspire science.

Advancing Suggestions Through Storytelling

Another technique Erickson used involved telling a story that appeared to be about someone else but was really directed to the person to whom he was speaking.

If you wanted to use this technique in a business context, you might say something like this to your prospect:

I'm not very good at sales. But the other day, I met this incredible little kid who wanted to sell me a bike. He was only about ten years old, but he had so much enthusiasm about that bike. He even said to me, "You know you're really going to want to buy from somebody like me because you know in your heart that I'm offering you a chance in a lifetime." I thought to myself, "It sure is funny and a little strange to hear that, but it's true." I mean, this kid was one helluva salesperson. I bought that bike.

Anyway, I'll never be as good at sales as that incredible kid, but I wondered, if you did purchase a pallet of my nine-cupped, fully adjustable brassieres for pregnant dogs, what color would you prefer, blue or green?

This is an insane example, but it makes the point. The idea is to tell a story that includes language you would like to say to your prospect directly but for various reasons cannot. For details, read *Uncommon Therapy* or consult books about Erickson listed at mischiefmarketing.com.

How the Mischief Marketing Tactics Work Together

As you get more and more adept at mischief marketing you'll see that many of the tactics I've discussed overlap a great deal. In fact, a really good mischief marketing campaign involves using almost all of these tactics to some degree. Together, they form a comprehensive mischief marketing strategy.

To illustrate this point, let's look at Philippe Kahn's story (Chapters 11 and 12) in terms of several discrete tactics.

Vulcan Tactic

You can say that Kahn used the Vulcan tactic because he never lied to the representative from *Byte* magazine. He simply made his office look busy and allowed the rep to infer that Borland was doing well.

You can use the Vulcan tactic without consciously prearranging anything the way Philippe did. In fact, that's often the best way to use it. For example, if at a party you happen to be standing next to a Rolls Royce, and if someone happens to assume the car belongs to you, and if you do nothing to confirm or deny that assumption because it's working to your advantage, then, even though you didn't deliberately set up the circumstances yourself, you're using the Vulcan tactic.

Wizard of Oz Tactic

You can say that Kahn used the Wizard of Oz tactic because the busy office made Borland look like a big, busy company. Unlike the Vulcan tactic, which often emerges from opportunity and accident, Wizard of Oz is always something you deliberately set up, as Kahn did in this case.

Playing up Your Faults

You can say that Kahn used the tactic of playing up his faults because when he told the *Byte* representative that he didn't have enough money to pay for an ad in *Byte*, he boldly highlighted something negative that the rep was probably already thinking anyway. By explicitly addressing that very thought, Kahn gained the man's trust to a far greater degree than he would have if he'd tried to act like a rich bigshot (which would have looked phony).

Percentage of Corporate Drones Likely to Mistakenly Believe that *Mischief Marketing* Does Not Apply to Them (Thank Heaven)

Mirroring Your Prospect

You can say that Kahn used the mirroring tactic because he made up those charts and graphs that the *Byte* rep "accidentally" spotted. Now, charts and graphs won't get you very far if your prospect is, let's say, an expert on ancient Celtic poetry. But they'll get you very far indeed if your prospect is a typical corporate drone. Charts and

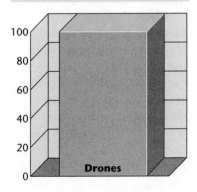

Drones

graphs mirror their communication style (speak their language). Here, for example, is a helpful chart that shows the percentage of corporate drones likely to believe mistakenly, thank heaven, that *Mischief Marketing* does not apply to them:

Kidding aside, don't ever make the mistake of assuming that, just because someone works for a corporation, they must be a corporate drone. This goes back to the judge not principle. In fact, some are actually geniuses who've figured out how to deal with the drones with whom they need to interact on a daily basis. Never forget that.

Getting Your Foot in the Door

You can say that Kahn used the getting your foot in the door tactic because the ad in *Byte* was his gateway to future success. And I think we can safely assume that anyone who would act as brashly as Kahn did must have been operating from a larger sense of life's meaning and purpose (living your myth).

Doing the Opposite of What's Expected

You can say that Kahn used this tactic, too, because he didn't ask the *Byte* rep to carry his ad. In fact, he made it look as though he had no interest in placing an ad with *Byte*.

We could supply many more such examples, but the point is clear: the primary mischief marketing techniques work together synergistically.

Take Martin Luther King's famous *I Have a Dream* speech, for example. You can tease out of that communication act any number of separate, discrete features that are nevertheless woven tightly together. You can talk about the variations in King's tone of voice, volume, and pacing. You can study the rhetorical devices he used, the Biblical allusions. You can focus on his gestures, facial expressions, the way his eyes got shiny with tears, the way he wavered slightly when he said "I may not get there with you." All these are separate, discrete fea-

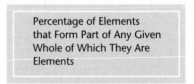

Percentage of Elements that Form Part of Any Given Whole of Which They Are Elements

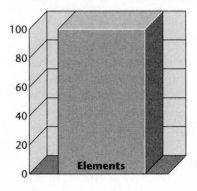

tures of the total communication, and yet each feature complements and reinforces the speech as a whole.

The same is true with any communication vehicle. The parts are separate, and yet they work together so closely that they're almost defined in terms of one another.

The chart on the previous page shows how parts relate to wholes in cases like this.

Mischievous Pop Quiz

1. **Mirroring your VLP means:**
   a) showering them with phony praise.
   b) using metaphors, phrases, styles of speaking, and other linguistic elements that are commonly employed in discussions of whatever excites your VLP's passion and interest—whether that's hockey, cooking, skiing, golf, macrame, the philosophy of Husserl, or whatever.
   c) taking every opportunity at board meetings to purse your lips and sing "Happy Birthday, Mr. President" slightly off key.

2. **People are often passionate about:**
   a) only what they're well known for doing professionally.
   b) almost anything but what they do professionally.
   c) for some incomprehensible reason, cooking; I wouldn't be surprised to learn that Yassir Arafat is proud of his skill as a cook.

3. **Some people prefer to think and talk about the world in the following ways, which you should reflect back to them if you're mischief marketing:**
   a) visually, in terms of images; as in, "See what I mean?"
   b) kinesthically, in terms of feelings and sensations; as in, "Get it?"
   c) aurally, in terms of hearing; as in, "Sound good to you?"
   e) in terms of Whitehead's metaphysical theory; as in, "Comprehend the concrescence of prehensions that underlies and defines each actual occasion, buddy?"
   f) all of the above, in varying proportions.

MEASURING
AND PARLAYING
YOUR RESULTS

In a conventional marketing campaign, you set measurable financial targets and dates. Then you use calendars, spreadsheets, project management software that works about as well as something Lucy
Ricardo might have designed, and a bunch of graphs, charts, and other
tools to determine whether or not you've met your projections.

Then you have a meeting about these charts and graphs with other
people in your company. Then you have another meeting. Then a middle manager who knows nothing about what you do—but a lot about
charts and graphs—starts hollering at you. This is because middle managers are masters of the Wizard of Oz tactic. Those who can't do, teach.
And those who can't even teach, tend to complain a lot.

Then you have another meeting. Then people start arguing. And sab-
otaging each other. Different departments go to war. Everyone in the
company gets demoralized. The middle manager's salary goes up.
Confusion reigns. Sooner or later, the company goes into the toilet for
good.

In a mischief marketing campaign, you have a few *primary* goals and
a number of *secondary* goals (which you defined in your marketing plan).
To determine whether you've achieved your primary goals, ask yourself
the following questions:

★ Did I follow the commandments?
★ Did I have a good time?
★ Did I avoid hurting anyone?
★ Did I help people in the course of this campaign?

If your answer to more than two of these questions is no, your campaign flopped. It doesn't matter if you made ten million dollars, it was
a dud. Go to work on the next one.

If Life Hands You Lemons . . .

Once, Ralph Hayles was both an ace attack-helicopter pilot and a commander of armored tanks. In other words, he was the kind of person who knew both the nuts-and-bolts stuff and the strategic stuff—a person blessed with a rare combination of both concrete and abstract combat skills. But sometimes, Ralph tried to do everything himself.

So it was that one day during the Gulf War, when Ralph was in charge of an elite strike force outfitted with missile-bearing Apache helicopters—a day when he was as usual trying to do everything himself—he suddenly lost everything.

What happened was this. Ralph was directing three Apaches on a mission to protect patrolling American vehicles. Radio scouts warned him of enemy forces nearby. Ralph calculated their positions on his computer and launched a pair of missiles. It seemed the right thing to do, but Ralph had made a terrible mistake. The missiles hit two of the U.S. vehicles he was supposed to protect.

The military never court-martialed Ralph, but they did strip him of his command. And, of course, his career was in ruins. For years, he couldn't stop brooding over his awful, tragic failure that day. He tried working as a stockbroker, but he hated selling over the phone. He tried to apply for jobs as an administrator, but various human resources denizens told him they couldn't hire him because of the publicity from the friendly-fire incident.

Married, with two little boys, Ralph soon ran through his savings. Did he sit around whining "Poor me?" Did he inauthentically dramatize his plight by saying, "Well, I deserve it! I'm going to shoot myself right now and let my wife and kids go to hell!" He did not.

Instead, Ralph sat down and created a marketable lesson for businesses. It was the lesson he had learned himself. It was about how to trust other people instead of trying to do everything yourself. On a lecture circuit where consulting experts usually talk about their successes and strong points, Ralph talked about his shortcomings. In a world where everyone usually tells you what to do, Ralph told you what *not* to do. In hotel conference rooms where everyone recycles the same upbeat ideas, Ralph brought new ideas.

In fact, he based an entire curriculum around what he had learned from his horrible experience. He turned everything around. Like a judo black belt, former army lieutenant colonel Ralph Hayles flipped failure into success. And in the process, he helped lots of other people avoid the same mistakes.

These days, Ralph's business has evolved to the point where it brings in about $360,000 a year in revenue. And his message has evolved, too. Although he started out drawing heavily on his Gulf War experience, he now delivers his lessons more often via teaching tales of great military leaders like Alexander, Napoleon, and Ulysses Grant.

And on some days, Ralph doesn't even mention the Gulf War. He doesn't have to any more.

Idea Joggers

- What defeats have you suffered in your life or in business?
- What did you learn from these experiences?
- Can you help others to learn what you learned?
- How can you parlay your failures into successes?

As for whether you achieved your secondary goals, that depends on what they were. For instance, in my case, after this book has been out for a while, I will ask myself the following questions:

★ Did I get to meet Judi Dench?
★ Did this book help someone to get started in business, to change careers, or to get across an important message?
★ Does Danielle talk to me for more than twenty minutes at a stretch?
★ Did I inspire my friend Chuck to finish his book?
★ Did I prove to Sheree that I can write a normal book proposal?
★ Did I get to work with Faith Popcorn?
★ Did I make Shira proud of her dorky dad?
★ Did I at least get her to clean up her room?
★ Did I succeed, somehow, in conveying to Irl and Myra that I now realize they're decent people after all?
★ Did I make my sister Ruth—who years ago inspired me to become a writer—finally think, "My brother did good"?
★ Did the book make enough money to get little Matthew the one, simple thing he wants for the holidays—his own Toys "R" Us?
★ Did it at least make enough to buy an action figure at Toys "R" Us?
★ Did I convince Elaine and Steve that they can set up slot machines dedicated to individual charities?
★ Did I get away from this computer long enough to find out who that gardener is that my kids are calling Daddy?

Guess what? It doesn't matter whether you achieve your secondary objectives or not. The judo tactic shows us why.

Parlaying Your Results: The Judo Tactic

Many good business and self-help books will tell you how to deal with failure, how to bolster your confidence, and so on. Again, visit mischiefmarketing.com for a list of these works. But I'm not going to talk much about how to deal with failure in this book because in mischief marketing, there is no such thing as failure. Everything gets put to good use. Everything gets recycled. Everything gets salvaged.

The following story illustrates what the judo tactic is all about.

Taylor Wines . . . His Tale to the Press

Winery founder Walter Taylor used mischief marketing judo to turn setbacks into successes.

It's been a crime for Walter Taylor to print his name on a bottle of wine since the Taylor Wine Company was bought by Coca-Cola in the mid-seventies. . . . [Taylor then went on to create a new wine, and Coca-Cola] ignored him until he began bragging about how his wine was the original, real Taylor, and then they successfully sued him for copyright infringement and unfair competition. Taylor had to remove his name from his wine labels; he couldn't even sign his own paintings that adorned them.

"They have stolen my birthright," he proclaimed on the courthouse steps. But he quickly capitalized on the affront. He handed out Magic Markers to his staff and a bunch of eager customers and had them black out the word "Taylor" wherever it occurred on his bottles of wine. The deleted name became the trademark he still uses, a way to keep alive his outrage.

The Coca-Cola Company was not amused. They sued again, and Walter Taylor was found in contempt of court. His reputation was by now made—a David battling the corporate Goliath. Courting the press, he used each new legal setback to his own advantage, and business boomed—sales of Bully Hill wine rose from $650,000 to $2 million during the two-year court battle.

. . . Taylor was a great showman whom tourists flocked to see at his vineyard wine tastings. He's explicitly spiritual about his work: "A product is an extension of a person's soul."

—DEBORAH TALL
From Where We Stand: Recovering a
Sense of Place
Knopf, 1993

Idea Joggers

- Don't be afraid that people might steal your ideas. This fear stops many wonderful people from achieving their dreams. Take the chance. Besides, you might be able to turn the theft around, the way author Barbara Chase-Riboud did when Dreamworks allegedly stole her novel to make the movie *Amistad*. As a result of her suit against the film company, Chase-Riboud won a lot of money.
- People stole lots of ideas from Walt Disney before he became famous. That didn't stop him, did it? Why should it stop you? We're talking about a guy with an idea about a large mouse. Aren't your ideas worth as much effort and perseverance as that man put into that rodent? Look at what he accomplished.
- Some companies are notorious for stealing ideas. What if you were to approach such a company pretending to be naive but actually being very savvy about documenting your interactions? Do you think a nice settlement from the company would help you start another business? Or would you rather expose its tactics publicly?
- Would it be just or unjust to mount your own sting operation and entice crooks into stealing your ideas? Careful with this!
- Be yourself. Are you a little odd, as Taylor was? So what? This is America, the land of opportunity. While you're poor and unknown, they'll call you crazy. But when you're rich, they'll call you eccentric. Enjoy yourself.

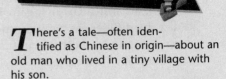

From the Pen to the Podium

A t the age of sixteen, Barry Minkow founded ZZZZ Best, a carpet-cleaning company that bilked investors for about $100 million back in the 1980s. In 1994, Barry was in the middle of serving a 7½-year prison sentence when Gary Zeune hired him (with the permission of a parole officer) to teach accountants how to detect financial impropriety. Why hire felons like Barry to teach accountants? The better to see fraud, my dear.

That was just the beginning. Not one to pass up a mischievous opportunity, Gary today runs a whole company based on judoing jailbirds into lecture-circuit jockeys. He stocks his stable of speakers by asking FBI agents he meets at his lectures to recommend other newly released white-collar criminals. One of his star speakers is former presidential confidant Webster Hubbell, currently under indictment for tax evasion and for deceiving federal investigators. Having served eighteen months of a twenty-one-month sentence, Hubbell is now on parole—and free to collect about $1,000 a talk through Gary's firm, Pros & Cons, a speaking troupe of white-collar criminals.

Not everyone is as lucky as Gary's speakers. Many ex-cons—even after paying their debt to society—have such a hard time finding good jobs that it's no wonder many (who would love to turn their lives around) end up turning back to crime to support themselves and their families. This is a situation in which everyone loses, including you and me. So let's hope that more people like Gary will shepherd others into using the mischief marketing judo tactic to do good things.

Barry Minkow, by the way, has since given up speaking and is now a minister.

—JOSHUA HARRIS PRAEGER
"Entrepreneur's Venture Puts Ex-Cons on the Podium"
Wall Street Journal Interactive Edition,
June 9, 1999

Good Luck or Bad?

T here's a tale—often identified as Chinese in origin—about an old man who lived in a tiny village with his son.

One night, the old man's only horse wandered off, so the neighbors dropped by to express how sorry they were about his bad luck. "How do you know it's bad luck?" he asked.

A week later, the horse returned, bringing along with him an entire herd of horses, thus making the old man the richest person in the village. The neighbors again dropped by, this time to congratulate him on his good luck. "How do you know it's good luck?" he asked.

When his son was thrown from one of the horses a few days later, the fall crippled the young man's leg. So the neighbors dropped by to offer their condolences. "How do you know this is bad luck?" the old man asked.

A while later, military officials came by to draft all able-bodied men into a war from which many would never return. Because the old man's son was crippled, he was spared. So the neighbors . . .

Idea Joggers

- Can you think of an event in your life that seemed at the time like a triumph but eventually led you into dangerous or unhealthy territory?

- Can you think of an event in your life that seemed like a defeat at the time but eventually led you to something good?

The point of the old man's tale is that your mischief marketing campaigns are going to be so deeply rooted in your unique personality—so grounded in your unknowable, individual destiny—that nobody else can really tell you what to do, what your results may ultimately mean, or what your work may eventually lead you to discovering.

For years, John Gray ran seminars about relationships (he still does). One day, much to his embarrassment, his own marriage started to fall apart. But instead of giving up, he and his wife sat down together and studied the differences between their communication styles. Their efforts to understand each other eventually led to the bestseller *Men Are from Mars, Women Are from Venus.*

Stop talking about that book! It's nothing but a bunch of cheap generalizations! And it's a bestseller so it can't possibly be any good. So what if it makes good points and helps people? Throw the baby out with the bathwater, that's what I say.

—RANDOM CRITICAL PSEUDO-INTELLECTUAL DEMON FROM HELL

Many successes are really products of failure—or of what looked like failure at first glance. Ivory Soap, for example, was born because somebody made a mistake at the soap factory. Penicillin was discovered because somebody didn't properly store a petri dish. And Columbus thought he was a failure when he stumbled upon America because he had his heart set on getting to India.

You've heard the old business saw: "Find a need and fill it." What is a need, however, but an area in which people are failing, or at least not doing as well as they'd like? In a very broad sense, therefore, every good offering represents an application of the judo tactic.

A successful man is one who can lay a firm foundation with the bricks that others throw at him.

—SIDNEY GREENBERG

Here's an important question to consider: Do we ever really know, at the moment when it occurs, whether a particular event represents a failure or a success?

Some Partying Words

If you've engineered a good mischief marketing campaign, if you've defined multiple goals, exit strategies, and knight forks; if you've created a mission statement, had fun, and accomplished something you can be proud of; if you've made the most of your resources; turned your life around; done some good work; immersed yourself in researching the lives and concerns of others instead of dwelling on your own; if you've grappled with inner and outer demons and seen through their attempts to trick you into taking your problems personally; if you've advanced at least one small step to detoxify yourself from our culture's addiction to money; if you've lightened up and lightened others up; if you've studied the commandments and stockpiled the abundance of mischievous weapons available to you; measured your results and determined how to judo them when necessary; if you now see that some of the most successful people in the world have had to wrestle with the very same things that bother you; and, finally, if you've made it to the end of the book, and perhaps already started on your own mischief marketing campaign, then congratulations.

For verily I say unto you that in the hall of fame, on the historical roster of presidents, painters, executives, publishers, biochemists, directors, actors, saints, sinners, comics, physicists, poets, mathematicians, martyrs, mavens and masters of mischief marketing you, too, shall be recognized—as a nut.

Welcome to the club.

INDEX

Lauder, Estée, 89–90
Letter-writing campaigns, 70–71
Level of recognizable effectiveness (LORE), 109–11
Lewis, Rudy, 101
Liberace Gambit, 122
Librarians, 45–46
Linguistic mirroring, 183–86
    advanced techniques for, 188–90
    for speech patterns, 187–88
Loaves and fishes tactic, 76
Loe, Marc, 172
Looking your best, 122–24
LORE (level of recognizable effectiveness), 109–11
Loud Records, 19
Lunar prospects, 54
Lundstrom, Meg, 150–51
Lying, mischief marketing and, 9
    commandment for, 119–21

M
Man's Search for Meaning (Frankl), 143
Marcus, Bernard, 92
Marketing. *See also* Mischief marketing
    comarketing, 131
    kamikaze, 123
    one-to-one, 72
    street, 19
    totalitarian, 23
    viral, 68
Martian prospects, 56
Mercurial prospects, 54–55
Merrick, David, 102–3
Metro Services Group, 43–44
Microsegmentation, 72
Miller Brewing Company, 14–15
Minkow, Barry, 199
Mirroring, 183–86, 191–92
    advanced techniques for, 188–90
    for speech patterns, 187–88
Mischief marketers
    authentic vs. inauthentic, 131
    Internet tools for, 61–70
    non-Internet tools for, 70–72
Mischief marketing
    astrology and, 51–58
    authentic, 12

One-to-one marketing, 72
Onlyborns, mischief marketing and, 49